Religion and the Scientific Future

 # ROSE—Reprints of
Scholarly Excellence

Certain good books should be, like the rose, not only hardy perennials in their intrinsic worth and usefulness, but also perennial in their availability. The purpose of the ROSE series is to make available such choice books from the past that are not otherwise available.

ROSE is intended primarily to meet the needs of the university classroom. Volumes are included in the series upon the recommendation of professors in the classroom who indicate a need for a currently out-of-print text. When investigation indicates that a reprint is warranted and available, ROSE reprints the text in an attractive and durable, yet affordable, format—equal or even superior to the original in quality.

Roses come in many varieties. So do books in the ROSE series. ROSE is not restricted to any one subject area but will reprint classics from any and all classes—the humanities, the sciences, the arts. But each is a "rose" of a reprint—preeminent among its kind, rare, of scholarly excellence.

RELIGION AND

THE SCIENTIFIC FUTURE

Reflections on Myth, Science, and Theology

by LANGDON GILKEY

Mercer University / ROSE
MUP Press
Macon, Ga. 31207

Religion and the Scientific Future, by Langdon Gilkey.

Copyright © 1970
by Langdon Gilkey.

Reprinted by arrangement with
Harper & Row, Publishers, Inc.

All Mercer University Press books are produced on acid-free paper
which exceeds the minimum standards set by
the National Historical Publications and Records Commission.

Library of Congress Cataloging in Publication Data
Gilkey, Langdon Brown, 1919-
    Religion and the scientific future.

    (ROSE ; no. 2)
    Reprint. Originally published: New York, Harper & Row, 1970 (The
Deems lectures ; 1967)
    Includes bibliographical references and index.
    1. Religion and science—1946—   —Addresses, essays, lectures.
I. Title.   II. Series.   III. Series: Deems lectures ; 1967.
BL241.G54   1982   291.1'75   81-18934
ISBN 0-86554-030-6   AACR2

For

FROUWKJE TJAKIEN RACHAEL GILKEY

THE DEEMS LECTURES

The Reverend Charles Force Deems, born in 1820, was deeply concerned with the relationship of science and philosophy to religion. In 1881 he founded the American Institute of Christian Philosophy for the investigation of the most significant questions pertaining to this relationship. In 1895, two years after the death of Dr. Deems, the American Institute of Christian Philosophy endowed a Lectureship of Philosophy at New York University in his honor and for a continuation of the purpose for which the institute had been founded.

Dr. Langdon Gilkey's lectures were sponsored by the Deems Fund, and were delivered in 1967.

About the Author

Langdon Gilkey is Shailer Mathews Professor of Theology at the Divinity School, University of Chicago. Professor Gilkey studied philosophy at Harvard College (B.A., 1940), and went from there to Yenching University in Peking where he taught English until his arrest by the Japanese on 8 December 1941. In March 1943 he was interned along with about 2,000 others in Shantung Province (see his *Shantung Compound*) until the end of World War II. Upon his return to the United States, Professor Gilkey turned his attentions to theology and studied at Union Theological Seminary, Columbia University (Ph.D., 1954), and as a Fulbright Fellow (1950-1951), at Cambridge in England. In 1954 he joined the theology faculty at Vanderbilt Divinity School where he became chairman of the department of theology, which post he left in 1963 to join the faculty at Chicago.

Langdon Gilkey has been recognized as "a thoughtful commentator on the confrontation of Christianity and secularization,"[1] and a "competent spokesman" for the "empirical movement in Christian theology,"[2] whose writings are filled with "illuminating insights and pioneering thoughts."[3] He has contributed many essays and articles to the various

---

[1] *The Great Ideas Today 1967* (Chicago: Encyclopedia Britannica Inc, 1967), p. 238.

[2] Edward Wing, in a review of *Religion and the Scientific Future*, in *The Christian Century* 87:33 (19 August 1970): 998.

[3] John D. Godsey, in a review of *Naming the Whirlwind*, in *The Christian Century* 87:23 (10 June 1970): 729.

theological journals over the years, and is the author of a number of important books, including *Maker of Heaven and Earth* (1959), *How the Church Can Minister to the World Without Losing Itself* (1964), *Naming the Whirlwind: The Renewal of God-Language* (1969), and *Message and Existence: An Introduction to Christian Theology* (1979). "There is no theological writing in America," one reviewer observed, "more profitable to read than Prof. Gilkey's."[4]

----

[4] Ibid.

Contents

Preface

The first three chapters of the four which make up this book were initially given at New York University in March 1967 under the auspices of the Deems Lectures referred to opposite the title page. Thus this volume is to be regarded as the publication of an enlarged and slightly revised version of those lectures. Subsequent to that delivery, the third lecture was reworked into its present form, incorporating motifs first explored in a paper entitled "Modern Myth-Making and the Possibilities of Twentieth Century Theology," and delivered at the Congress on Theology of the Renewal of the Church on the occasion of the Centenary of Canada in August 1968 (cf. *Theology of Renewal*, L. K. Shook ed., Montreal, Palm Publishers, 1968, Vol. I, pp. 283–312). Later the fourth chapter was added to these three; and then this new compound of many materials was organized in a new way for the Cole Lectures at the Divinity School of Vanderbilt University in April 1969.

The author would like to express here his gratitude to the members of the Deems Committee for their invitation to expound this general subject and their continuing cooperation in securing its publication; to the hosts and confreres at the lustrous Congress in Toronto; and to my colleagues and friends at Vanderbilt: in the Divinity School, in the physics and philosophy departments, the bookstore and the community generally, who for ten years and now at each return have made it such stimulating fun to be there. I wish also to thank Mrs. Anne Grant and Mrs. Sonya Illianova for their excellent and patient typing of the manuscript, and James Yerkes for his great help in checking the references and preparing the index. This volume is dedicated to our daughter who made her appearance in our world on the date below.

LANGDON GILKEY

October 29, 1969
The Divinity School
The University of Chicago

Religion and the Scientific Future

I. The Influence of Science
on Recent Theology

THE THEME IN THESE CHAPTERS is the mutual influence and, as we see it, the mutual dependence of science and theology. The thread that will bind our discussion of the relations of science and theology together is the question of the meaning of mythical or religious discourse, its character, status, sources, and uses in a scientific culture. It is with regard to this question I believe, that on the one hand, the recent influence of science on religion has been most determinative; and it is here, on the other, that because of this influence, the most interesting and fruitful, if not devastating, theological problems of the present have arisen. In this opening chapter, we will consider the many significant ways recent science—that is, the science of the nineteenth and twentieth centuries—has influenced, often unbeknown to us in theology, our conceptions of what religious truth does and means.

For reasons we shall see later, in the recent theological past the massive influence of science on the character and status of theological talk has hardly been a popular point to emphasize. Theology has barely been prepared to admit the influence of philosophy on its understanding of religious truth, much less that of science. Picturing real or valid theology as an autonomous (that is, noncultural) discipline dependent only on its own sources of divine revelation and responding faith, neo-orthodox or Biblical theology sought to understand itself solely on its own "revelational"—or, as I would rather say, "religious"—terms, and thus did not recognize the immense impact developments in science made on its self-understanding. And this in large part, as we shall try to show, accounts for its present state of exhaustion.

Of course, it is correct that changes in religious sensibility, especially vis-à-vis man and his destiny, new interpretations of the Bible, and new forms of church life have also been important influences on the understanding of religious truth; and surely developments in recent philosophy have had their own impact. Our thesis, however, is that the most important change in the understanding of religious truth in the last centuries—a change that still dominates our thought today —has been caused more by the work of science than by any other factor, religious or cultural.

The change referred to is that from the understanding of religious truths as made up of propositions containing, among other things, divinely revealed "information" on almost any topic of interest, to the understanding of them as a system of symbols which make no authoritative assertions about concrete matters of fact. Within the last century the mythical language of religion, which, when systematically reflected upon, becomes theological discourse, has relinquished the claim to be able to make indicative statements about matters of fact; in its place this language has seen itself as "solely myth," or "broken myth"—a form of language which, to my knowledge, is quite new in the history of religion. This raises peculiar problems about its own meanings, its usage, and of course its validity.

We cannot embark here upon any sort of satisfactory history of mythical and religious discourse. It is, I believe, safe to say that in all its original forms, such language was blatantly multivalent or polysemic in character. That is, while it spoke of the transcendent or the sacred—and this was its main purpose—it almost always spoke of the divine as it had manifested itself in and through some finite object, person, or event. There is, then, an inescapable "factual" or "matter-of-fact" element in all early myth.

Many myths appear linguistically simply as stories of past events; as the Dinka myth tells us, the hero came to a certain spot at a certain time and earned the fishing spear.[1] Or, to speak in our own lingo, Yahweh acted in certain observable and describable ways—apparently historical or "factual" in character—in creation, at the Flood, with the Patriarchs, and at the Exodus. From the factual or descriptive character of the language used, it was almost as if he were a being in space and time, doing deeds within that presupposed continuum. Only the sacred content of the story reveals its transcendent subject, one who *began* space and time and so who transcends them, and thus one who must in some way enter that continuum from beyond it in order to act within it.

As we have often been reminded by the students of scripture, the language of Biblical myth, as had the myths of other religious communities, told a story.[2] And the story: whether of what the divine beings did *in illo tempore* to establish the world, as Mircea Eliade says, or what Yahweh and his creature Adam did in the great and crucial events of the seminal past, was assumed to contain as a necessary element a set of indicative statements about natural and historical matters of fact. Even when these fundamental stories of the Christian tradition were partially transformed by philosophical speculation so as to contain ontological propositions—so that they could achieve the transcendence and the universality implicit in their own meanings—this factual side

or element of our doctrines or dogmas remained. God became transcendent being and not just a localized personal
being; but still what he did, whether in creation, judgment,
redemption, or eschatology, touched the realm of concrete
fact at a certain definable place and time in a reportable
event. Consequently, the theological narration of what he did
or promised to do, that is, the fundamental symbols of the
Christian tradition, included both the transcendent, universal elements and a concrete factual element. Adam may have
stood as a symbol for the universal possibilities and yet the
predicament characteristic of all men; nevertheless, as he
was for all classical theology[3]—and even for the early Rahner[4]
—he was also a particular man who had done a particular
deed at a given place and time.

Traditional religious language, and the theological language that represents reflection upon it, thus had two foci: a
transcending, universalizing element expressive of the sacred
dimension of the event narrated, usually borne in classical
theology by the philosophical elements within the propositions of theological discourse; and a concrete, matter-of-fact
element couched in the purely factual language of propositions ordinarily used to report and describe ordinary natural
or historical events. The complications caused by the role of
philosophical discourse in religious and theological language
so interpreted is a well-known theme, and too broad to be
broached here. Our present interest is in the history, or
"fate," if you will, of the *factual* element, for it is this which
science has successfully eradicated, once and for all, for good
or for ill, from our discourse.

It is perhaps safe to say further that although many other
important changes in the concept of religious truth have occurred in church history, for example in the process of Hel-
lenization in the early church, or in that of de-Hellenization
at the Reformation, nevertheless this particular one is per-

haps the most important of all. And happily or unhappily for us in theology, this quite fundamental change has occurred recently, in fact mostly in the last century. With all their debates about reason and revelation, neither the Reformers, nor most of the Enlightenment theologians, ever doubted that revelation was composed of objective propositions concerning matters of fact, that it could therefore tell us what had happened in space and time, and provide authoritative descriptions of the character, time, place, and causes of such concrete events as were crucial to the meaning of significant doctrines.

In fact, right up to the end of the eighteenth century, it was taken for granted that Biblical truth included all manner of statements about the age and early stages of the world's geological life, the creation of plants and animals, the making and the early history of man, important facts of relevant geography—as well as trustworthy statements about the sacred history on which our redemption depended. When we encounter, for example, in Luther's *Commentary on Genesis*, his interest in what the actual rivers were that flowed in and out of Eden,[5] we realize how different was his understanding of revelation and of the religious truth which was its result than is ours. And the shock is greater when Charles Gillispie tells us that in 1824 a clergyman—no fundamentalist at all, but a respected member of the Wernerian geological society— had as his special field of science "Biblical zoology."[6]

To be sure, in and through the developing Enlightenment some of the implications of modern science, then represented by Galilean and Newtonian mechanics, had been clearly seen for the *present* universe. Religious truths, it was generally agreed, did not deal with any *present* matters that came under the purview of physics or astronomy, and miracles within experienced history were certainly now suspect for many. Accordingly, in Enlightenment Deism, God's deeds were localized in the past, in the originating acts of creation, and in the future, in the eschatological judgments at the end.[7] The divine activity, and hence religious statements about it, was, so to speak, banished from the contemporary universe and moved safely out of the range of matters of fact then available to scientific inquiry. But with regard to the distant past, and the equally distant future, and especially with regard to statements about the origins and early history of the world, in which periods Enlightenment science had relatively little direct interest, religious truth was felt by all to be extremely relevant.

Consequently, most intelligent men, and so most scientists, held that divine revelation could tell us what had happened in the beginning, how the Creator had, so to speak, set the stage of the world which their science was now newly investigating.[8] Only certain perceptive philosophers and a few theologians, especially Kant,[9] Hegel, and Schleiermacher, saw in Enlightenment science a deep challenge to religious language as it was then understood, and sought to transform from the ground up the theoretical structure of that language. For most intellectual men, however, scientific or clerical (and they were often the same), religious truth was still information, albeit now about facts beyond our discovery, and, as authoritative, it presented us with certain knowledge of the origins, the ultimate framework, and the final destiny of the nature that science was seeking to understand.

Apparently, then, what finally caused the change in religious language we are tracing was not so much the method of modern science as a shift in the direction and character of its interests. Beginning at the end of the eighteenth and all during the first two-thirds of the nineteenth century a new cluster of sciences became dominant, namely geology, paleontology, and biology. It was around these that discussion and controversy swirled; they set the tone and raised the issues that interested intelligent men. The crucial point is that these newly dominant sciences were *historical*. Their method as they came to full development was to understand the structure and character of their subject matter by an understanding of its history. Thus what they gradually unfolded was a *story* of the earth and of its life which enthralled, captivated, and in part frightened early nineteenth-century minds. For the first time science provided a story of the early happenings of earth—and by implication a description also of its utopian ending—in direct controversy with the traditional story on the same subject provided by the Biblical history. When Copernican, Galilean, and Newtonian astronomy had taken away the view of the spatial realms of the universe implied in scripture, that was incidental to the Bible, which was in essence no geographical tract. But when the new sciences showed that the Biblical *history* was in error, that was something else again, and the understanding of what Biblical truth was had perforce to change. Archaeology, ancient history, physical anthropology, and many other historical sciences might have done the same thing; geology, paleontology, and biology came first, and thus to them goes this particular palm.

Let us now examine this history in more detail; it is brief, lasting roughly from 1780 or so to 1859. And yet in that short space of time all of our conceptions of our origins, of our own past, of that of the earth around us, and of what the Lord had or had not done in all of this, were completely overturned. And out of that confusion arose a quite new view of religious truth and thus of theological language which we all share.

At the beginning of this period, prior to 1750 or so, most scientists, outside of a very few, and most religious thinkers assumed with Francis Bacon[10] that knowledge of God was available to man in two forms: from "the Book of the Word," a knowledge which was gained by an exegesis of scripture, and from "the Book of Nature," a knowledge to be uncovered by the inquiries of science. Far from controverting each other, the information contained in each of these two arenas of inquiry supported and supplemented the other. It is, moreover, apparent that while for most sixteenth-century Christians God was more clearly and certainly seen in the Word than in nature, later this balance tended to shift. The knowledge of God in the order and adaptation of nature, so evident to the seventeenth- and eighteenth-century mind, enthralled with Newtonian mechanics, was increasingly the primary source for believers' certainty of God's existence.[11] And, as the eighteenth-century debates about the use or uselessness of revelation show, for not a few the knowledge of God through nature had become the only relevant source of our knowledge of his power, and even of his benevolence.[12]

However, for most important scientists and thinkers, the significance of revealed knowledge was by no means negligible, and not least within the general area of our knowledge of nature; the knowledge of God in the Word helped us to understand the work of God in nature. For as was commonly held, divine revelation provided certain sorts of information about God's activity in the cosmos which were both necessary to scientific understanding and yet beyond the reach of scientific investigation. In effect, what revelation did was to provide the widest cosmological framework within which the science of the time understood itself. This revealed knowledge, relevant to science, meant two sorts or bodies of knowledge.

1. There was the knowledge of the act of creation. Not, to be sure, *how* creation had been accomplished, for this would be unintelligible to mankind. Rather what revelation told us was *that* it had been done and by whom; done, that is, in a

recent act, effective for all subsequent history, and done by a wise, beneficent deity according to a rational and purposive plan. Although this knowledge of the creation of the natural world by the divine wisdom was implied in the orderliness and economy of nature, it was made certain to our minds only by the revelation of scripture.[13]

This view of the beginning of things was, moreover, the crucial cosmological presupposition of most of current scientific inquiry; it provided the most general framework in which the scientific assumptions of the time made sense. These assumptions, reinforced by all of science from Galileo through Newton, Priestley, Ray, Dalton, Boyle, and Thomas Burnett even down to Linnaeus and Cuvier, were: (a) That the fundamental forms and structures of present natural things had been permanently established by a recent act of creation, and thus that the laws concerning these permanent forms or species were universal and timeless. (b) That these permanent forms made up an intelligible system in relation to their world because they were purposefully or teleologically preadapted to each other and to their environment by the wisdom and benevolence of the Creator in a glorious harmony of ends and means.

These two assumptions: that permanent forms had been created at the beginning by God, and that therefore the harmony of these was the work of his benevolent purpose, were alone able to account for the character of Enlightenment science. For that science was, first of all (for example, by Ray and Linnaeus in biology[14]), a search for *invariant* forms of *permanent* species of which all the varieties of natural life were but inexact illustrations. Secondly, they were alone able to explain the sense of the harmony of such science and religion, so pervasive in the scientific societies of the period. On this assumption alone could it be intelligible that the inquiries of physicists, astronomers, and biologists, by uncovering the harmony of the universe, would serve to reveal rather than to obscure the glory of its Creator. In *this* cosmological context (and in it alone) a discovery of mechanical harmony seemed to validate (and did not invalidate) a teleological foundation for things. Ironically, in the Darwinian context that was to follow, it was precisely a similar discovery of universal mechanism which overwhelmed teleology. The difference lies in the assumption that the harmony discovered was a harmony established by extranatural power and so necessarily by a supernatural Creator at the beginning of all things.

Needless to say, all these men who regarded such revealed knowledge as providing the fundamental presuppositions for their own scientific inquiry, thought of the divine event of creation thus known as an event in spatiotemporal continuity with the natural history they were investigating. For them the *religious* knowledge of creation was in continuity with the *scientific* knowledge of species because the former provided the intelligible explanation for the origin of the same species they were in their researches concretely investigating.

2. As the eighteenth century moved on, furthermore, another sort of truth of revelation joined this knowledge of the act of creation as relevant to science. With the gradual growth of geological speculation in the seventeenth and eighteenth centuries, it became apparent that not only was more time necessary for earth's history to develop than the 6,000 years traditional in Biblical exegesis. It seemed now certain that fundamental changes in the earth itself had occurred during the course of that development, and after the originating act of creation. The history implied in fossil remains, only gradually understood, was one in which vast changes had obviously occurred, both in the earth's character and in its kinds of plants and animals.

We are quite accustomed to this "fact"—we know that the early terrain of our globe was utterly different from its present character, and that countless weird forms of life, now extinct, have in the millennia since roamed over this changing surface.

These "facts" came as a tremendous shock to the European mind, and they raised innumerable questions. If such giant changes had happened, why had no histories, even our sacred history, recorded them—unless the earth were much older than man and his history books? And if such an unbelievably long history of profound changes was beginning undeniably to reveal itself in the earth, how was this process of change to be understood on the most fundamental level? Had God caused it; and if so, how? If not, what *had* caused it, and where was God meanwhile? Certainly Buffon, LaPlace, and other French materialists, following rigorously the implications of the Cartesian and Newtonian view that all that happens in nature reflects merely the history of matter in motion, saw no problem either in explaining such changes or in understanding what God had been about—deity had for them long vanished from relevance to scientific explanation. Nevertheless, most men of that time still assumed that religious knowledge was both true and also directly of one piece with scientific knowledge. Thus as the scientific knowledge of the past grew, serious problems arose for them. How was God's activity in the course of events, guaranteed by revelation and supposedly affirmed as well by scientific inquiry, related to this new and somewhat terrifying history of geological change, and in turn, how were these cataclysmic changes to be understood in terms of what we knew through other sources of the divine activity?

One answer, first seriously suggested by John Woodward in 1695, a man early aware of the great significance of fossils, was that the only way to account for the giant cataclysms and changing types of life that the fossils seemed to imply, was by certain great acts of divine intervention in the course of nature, preeminently the Flood referred to in scripture. It seemed intelligible to hold that God had, as in the case of the Flood, intervened in nature's "normal" processes in massive destructive and creative activity and thus effected the apparent transformations of earth and of its life recorded in the rocks. For to the science of this time, these changes in organic life were serious anomalies, anomalies, that is, since they challenged the universally assumed theory of permanent forms established at the beginning which we have mentioned. Thus began the tradition of "catastrophic geology," so popular and powerful for one hundred years until it was finally disposed of in 1830 by the publication of Charles Lyell's work founding modern scientific geology.

The essence of the position of catastrophic geology is very relevant to our theme. According to this view, the scientific history of the earth and of its forms of life, which undoubtedly had undergone vast changes, could be understood only in terms of a series of catastrophic divine acts—"mighty acts of God," one might say.[15] The miraculous character of these mighty acts is well illustrated by the remark of Cuvier, the great paleontologist, in 1812, explaining the events that had removed those species which once roamed the earth but are now nowhere present: "The thread of operations is here broken, the march of nature is changed, and none of the agents that she now employs were sufficient for the production of her ancient works."[16] And, of course, if the processes of nature were thus interrupted by supernatural agency, scientific inquiry on the basis of normal, present processes could tell us nothing of the causes of these fundamental eruptions.

In his inaugural lecture in 1819 as professor of geology at Oxford, Cuvier's disciple William Buckland emphasized the continuity between the Biblical accounts of God's mighty

acts so understood, and the theories of most modern geological scientists. The point of his lecture, said he, was "to shew
that the study of geology has a tendency to confirm the evidences of natural religion; and that the facts developed by it
are consistent with the accounts of the creation and deluge
recorded in the Mosaic writings."[17] Although now the Mosaic
six days had of necessity been allegorized into a much longer
time span, still the accounts in scripture of God's mighty
acts, ending with the Flood, were here regarded as providing
the necessary "factual" framework of historical events within which geology could understand its own strange data.
While, said Buckland, the scientific geologist could help us to
understand scientifically the *effects* of these divine acts
through geology's explications of the fossils and of the rock
strata, still, apparently, revelation alone could tell us of their
divine *causes*. Thus an apparently quite scientific, "scriptural" geology appeared as a major school of that science,
championed by many of Europe and England's leading scientists during the first part of the nineteenth century.

We ourselves are not unfamiliar with this understanding
of religious truth as directly relevant to, as of one piece with,
scientific data. The difference is that we find it now only in
the more bizarre elements of our culture, for example, when
present-day Fundamentalists are delighted at discovering a
scientific account in accord with the Biblical stories; or whenever a scientific explanation for such "Biblical facts" as the
sun that stopped for Joshua is presented triumphantly to us.
The vast change that has occurred in the understanding of
the nature of revelation and of religious truth during the
last 150 years is well revealed by our own utter certainty
that this sort of combination of revealed truth and scientific
truth makes no sense, that the forms of discourse represented
by religious language and by scientific language are not to be
so directly and easily mixed together. The brew that scientific professors contentedly mixed in the early nineteenth

century is such that even parsons and theological students in the twentieth refuse to drink!

Unless I am way wide of the mark, for us religious knowledge of God's action, whether expressed in mythical language or in the reflective semiphilosophical discourse of theology, is not in direct continuity with scientific knowledge. We do not think it can function as a part of a coordinated system of scientific or historical knowledge of the space-time system of things, even as its initiatory chapter,[18] nor can it directly fill in any gaps there may currently be in that system.

This position, so unquestionably assumed by all of us, was for the first time definitely established by the controversy in geology we are describing. Cataclysmic geology was the last serious attempt on the part of scientists to use religious knowledge as an essential part of their own system of understanding. Thus in the victory over this form of geology by its rival, uniformitarianism, the principle of the distinction between the kind of truth science offers us and the kind that religion might provide was made a fundamental, and unavoidable, presupposition for all subsequent theological self-understanding.

Uniformitarianism insisted, as Charles Lyell said, "that *all* former changes of the organic and inorganic creation are referable to one uninterrupted course of physical events, governed by the laws now in operation."[19] That is to say, as far as geological science was concerned, no divine interventions, no "mighty acts of God," were either relevant or necessary to a full explanation of all the earth's changes. Since, moreover, Lyell was in fact able to explain all major geological changes according to the principle of currently observable causes understood by currently known laws,[20] the hypothesis of the divine activity either within geological explanation or as one of its direct presuppositions vanished.

As an immediate consequence, revealed truths were separated from all scientific accounts of the earth's development. And no longer was the Biblical Flood ever conceived as the basis for any geological explanation. Such an unusual flood might have happened, to be sure; but if that were so, such an event would now be explained by the universal and mechanistic principles of geology. It would not itself become the basis for *their* explanation. The Flood became at best an illustration of scientific law, not its transscientific foundation. One important kind of religious truth relevant to science, namely a religious knowledge of God's "mighty acts" during the course of nature's development, thus disappeared from science. Henceforth theology was no longer conceived as providing any special information useful to the pursuits of any branch of physical science.

If in this way God's acts within nature seemed to be driven from scientific inquiry, how fared now the other sort of religious information believed to be relevant to science? We refer to the revealed knowledge of the originating divine creation of the permanent forms of life. Even Lyell, who understood so clearly that religious knowledge must be separated from geology, still held that the divine creative activity was the sole means through which the origins of man might be understood.[21] The pious among the uniformitarians—and there were many—had long said that while religious truth had no relation to the story of subhuman *nature*, it did concern directly the history of Man: his origins, his duties, and his destiny. Along with most other scientists in the early nineteenth century, Lyell and his friends continued to believe that science could not explain in terms of law the origins of the forms of life, and especially of man's life. Rather, these could be explicated only as structures *given* to our investigation from beyond the range of inquiry, that is, as forms created directly by God. Theology alone therefore could explain the *origin* of species; the task of science was to classify and describe the varieties so formed.

As we know, the work of Charles Darwin changed all this.

After him it was plain to men educated in, and concerned with, science—and so to liberal theologians as well—that religious knowledge had no more direct connection with any aspect of biological theory than it did with geology. Thus the explication of the origin of the forms of life became a *secular* inquiry for biology to pursue, not a *religious* inquiry to be resolved by exegesis and theological injunction. Darwin showed that for the purposes of biology, a naturalistic as opposed to a theological explanation even of the origins of species was possible and sufficient. Perhaps his greatest achievement was to apply to the changing history of life itself the scientific principle of uniformitarianism, and therefore to explain by natural causes now operative in present experience, plus random mutations, the transformations that that history had undergone. In his hands uniform laws became the exhaustive explanation, as far as science was concerned, of organic development, and there was no place left for religious information to be useful to cognitive inquiry into biological subjects.

Henceforth, for any person accepting science as providing the normative mode of knowing the space-time world and its history—and this included most members of the intelligentsia, even we ourselves—this verdict of the scientific community about divine revelation and biology effectively removed religious truth from the area of matters of fact. From then on no serious theologian, in the Protestant world at least, has claimed that through some form of religious knowing he could establish anything relevant to the data or the conclusions of scientific inquiry—and, as a consequence, even of historical inquiry.

Since the nineteenth century, then, theology has understood itself to possess no legitimate ground to interfere with either scientific inquiry or scientific conclusions, whether in the fields of natural or of historical inquiry. Theology has rightly continued to believe that natural processes and historical events—particularly certain "special" events—were in some significant regard relevant to, perhaps even crucial for, religious and theological language—as in the paradigmatic cases of the Exodus and of Jesus of Nazareth. What was now unarguable was that any certainty concerning these processes or events, either as having in fact happened or how they happened, was a matter for scientific or historical inquiry and thus could not be deduced from dogmatic or theological truths. Theological truths no longer contained the sort of knowledge which entails particular factual propositions. Belief in the Incarnation might well require that there have been a Jesus if it were to be a meaningful belief; but such belief did not in itself guarantee or entail certainty about the historical existence and life of Jesus.

Thus were the two elements of theological language—its transcending aspects pointing to ultimacy and sacrality, to the actions of God, and its factual aspects—separated for the first time. And it was the claim of science, a claim accepted by all liberals, exhaustively on its own terms to provide explanatory knowledge of spatiotemporal matters of fact, that effected this separation. Strangely enough, even the most "intramural" problems of recent theology, especially the question of the relation of the historical Jesus to the Christ of proclamation, have arisen as problems under the influence of an aspect of modern culture far removed in spirit from the pious albeit scholarly study of New Testament texts, namely the work of scientific inquiries into nature which divested belief and theological propositions alike of their ability to guarantee factual propositions. And thus did theological statements about God and his activities become what we now call "sheer myth" or "broken myth,"[22] symbol qua symbol.[23] While as forms of language these "symbols" or "myths" may well embody in their eidetic meanings refer-

ences to certain facts or events, nevertheless they are such
that faith in the symbol or the myth, and affirmation of its
truth, no longer assure one of the happening of any facts connected with the myth or inform one of the character of these
facts. *What* these myths might now mean, if thus shorn of
their power to make factual assertions, was left for the liberal theology of the nineteenth century and almost all the
theology of our time somewhat anxiously to explore, and for
us to discuss in the next three chapters.[24]

This was, I believe, the uncomfortable process by which
the affirmation of a religious truth was separated from indicative assertions of matters of fact, and in which it became in
that sense "purely symbolic." If the thought now occurs that
"it's about time religion understood its language as symbolic,
and so as neither literal nor directly applicable to reality 'out
there,' " it is well to recall that it was almost another hundred
years, with the beginning of quantum physics at the turn of
the twentieth century, that physics began to become aware of
the peculiar way in which its discourse is symbolic.[25]

In any case, most of nineteenth-century theology was based
on this new understanding of religious truth as symbolic
rather than as containing literal, propositionally revealed information. The liberal theologians were very much aware of
these mounting tensions between science and religion, and
deliberately fashioned their new understanding of religion
in the light of this history. For as their whole century witnessed,[26] Christians were now faced with a new and urgent
problem: If religious truth is not made up of objective propositions informing us of facts, events, and their causes—and
when it tries to do so, seems always to be wrong—what *does*
it tell us of, what does it mean, what kind of truth is it? The
liberal theologies of Schleiermacher, of the Ritschlian moral-
ists, of the Hegelian idealists, and of the Whiteheadian
processors—to name a few—have provided various answers

to this question: religious truth is reflection on direct religious or Christian experience; since it concerns the implications of moral experience, it is based on value judgments; or it is an intuitive, emotive, imaginative, therefore pictorial form of philosophical and metaphysical truth about the world —or, as Feuerbach insisted, it is a false projection of man's unique powers onto the omnipotent power of nature.[27] None of these regard the propositions of religious truth as directly concerned with, or entailing, any set of empirical or scientific facts; for all of them science alone—and not any form of religious truth—can tell us anything of the observable phenomenal world, of the characteristics of the realm of things in space and time, of what has been called the realm of secondary causation.

Two results of this separation, so important in nineteenth-century liberal theology, might be mentioned. By thus leaving the phenomenal realm of space-time fact open to science, liberal theology raised for science and for a scientific culture a very important contemporary question: Is the scientific type of explanation then final? If science alone can tell us the spatiotemporal facts, and if religious truth cannot sneak in between these facts as a "scientific-type hypothesis," does this mean that religious truth has *no* function, that all is exhaustively explained when it is scientifically explained, that in a scientific culture there is consequently no need for religious knowledge and no meaning to religious truth? Obviously the same question has been baffling philosophy about *its* truth[28]—and for many of the same reasons. And secondly, the related question arises: If religious knowledge of the divine activity is not relevant to a scientific understanding of past and present events in nature or in history, does this mean that there was and is no divine activity at all, that God's hand is removed from the actual course of the world?

In general, liberal religion answered this last question

about God and the cosmos by saying that though God's acts no longer entered directly into the phenomenal realm of secondary causation, and so neither provided any miracles on the one hand nor were a part of any scientific inquiry on the other, still God's rule over the world's order could be understood as an implication of the very story science had unfolded. For that story was one of a marvelous *development* of forms in a *progressive* direction. Thus religion in a scientific age could still speak of the divine activity behind and within the changes traced by science, an activity that accounted for the obvious development of things toward higher and higher forms of life, of culture, of morals, and of religion. "God" was the religious symbol of the creative force making for progress. Religious truth, although no longer a part of science, was thus one of the strongest implications of scientific inquiry. For in the nineteenth century both the scientific study of nature and the historical study of mankind's development alike seemed to reveal to the discerning eye the guiding hand of purpose, and of divine providence.

It was surely one of history's ironies that Darwin, who had somewhat ruthlessly disposed of Paley's God, the great engineer and the grand artificer of man at the beginning, was to find the liberal's immanent God of inevitable progress resurrected on the basis of his own naturalistic theory of evolution.[29] In the struggle for the survival of the fittest in a changing cultural environment, the figure of God seemed to have more existential staying power, more evolutionary potential, than Darwin had ever guessed He possessed!

It might seem, then, that in its first round with recent science, religion had been pummeled but not beaten, for it had reappeared in the second round, perhaps in an even stronger form because based now on the new scientific understanding of nature and history as an evolving process. This resuscitation was, however, relatively brief. In the twentieth century the theory of cosmic and historical progress on which most liberal theology based its religious language about God itself disintegrated. History appeared far too turbulent, ambiguous, and continuously creative of new evil to be called "progress." Thus if the modern man's God be termed the "creative force driving events toward value or the good," that liberal God seemed as hidden to twentieth-century eyes as was the intervening God of pre-Darwinian days. Evolution, now reduced by twentieth-century experience to a lower-case word, remained, to be sure, a respected theory in biology. Generally speaking, however, it was no longer viewed as the key that unlocked the ultimate mystery of cosmic and historical change.

In the twentieth century, all those secular "places" where God's activity or presence had seemed obvious to the nineteenth-century mind now appeared to be devoid of traces of deity. Scientific and historical studies of the past, taken on their own terms, were to most biologists and historians vacant of evidence of overarching divine purpose; man's morality seemed as corrupt as ever, his history chaotic and directionless, and his religious experience tinged with fanaticism or despair. Nowhere in ordinary experience could the moral and purposive God of nineteenth-century experience seem to be available. As the growth of early nineteenth-century *science* had separated the activity of God from natural events and thus from scientific inquiry, hypotheses, and conclusions, so the turmoil of twentieth-century *history* seemed to remove all traces of God from the historical experience of man. If, then, in the twentieth century, neither natural process nor historical experience could reveal the work of God, where could religious truth be based, and what might it now say?

The answer is well known to us all. In the neo-orthodox

theology that has dominated twentieth-century Protestant-
ism until almost yesterday, religious truth was founded not
on the word of man about the general processes of either nature or history, but on the Word of God in scripture. Thus in
no sense was religious language, in theory at least, derived
from scientific inquiry nor even significantly related to it.
With regard to the knowledge of God the Book of Nature for
neo-orthodoxy was permanently closed, and the Book of History too ambiguous to read without the spectacles of faith.[30]
Consequently, only the Book of Revelation of God's special
acts in history could witness to the Lord and his works. The
separation between factual propositions and religious statements, established by scientific development and liberal
religion, was thus accepted and reformulated by neo-orthodoxy to express its own understanding of religious truth
within the limits set by an increasingly secular culture. For
them, therefore, scientific and historical language, while perfectly valid in their own context, dealt with the observable,
discoverable, and verifiable network of relations among creatures, with the realm of finite natural or human causes, or (to
use Tillich's phrase) with the subject-object dimension of
experience.

Religious language, on the other hand, the language
evoked in response to God's revelation, concerned another
dimension entirely, the relation of the creaturely to the
transcendent, or better, the creative and real activity of the
transcendent within the history of the creaturely.[31] This activity was neither phenomenal nor observable, though it was
real, and thus no scientific or philosophical inquiry into nature or history could possibly uncover it or describe it. On
the contrary, we can hear of God's acts, and through them of
God, only through the witness of the Word in scripture, and
we ourselves can know of them, "see" them, and witness to
them only through our responding faith. Between the two

realms of theological statements and scientific inquiry there is no possible conflict because there is no interrelationship or mutual dependence. Theology is autonomously based on revelation and faith alone; and when it is true to itself, it unfolds its concepts independently of the fluctuations of scientific theories about nature, or of historical speculations about what did or did not happen in the past.[32]

Whereas most liberal theologians had eagerly studied cosmology, biology, and history, and had based their theological constructions on the wider implications of these scientific theories, quite to the contrary the neo-orthodox were conspicuously indifferent to scientific theories and hostile to any of their theological implications. What extracurricular readings they did in secular disciplines were at most in psychotherapy, history, and possibly sociology, and they were inclined to emphasize the "nonscientific," the "existential," and the personalistic character of these, their favorite disciplines.[33] To be sure, none of them ever doubted evolution as a biological theory (nor the propriety of its being taught in public schools!), nor did they dream of questioning the legitimacy, say, of archaeological or historical studies of the Biblical periods. On the other hand, none of them considered using the biological theory of evolution as the basis for a *theological* concept of creation or providence; nor was anyone perturbed over the controversy between the astronomical "big bang" theory of cosmic creation and astrophysicist Fred Hoyle's speculation about continuing creation. And until Moltmann and Pannenberg, no one conceived that historical inquiry could again be a ground for a Christology based on the Resurrection!

On the whole, the neo-orthodox pictured themselves as writing theology only from the faithful study of scripture and of church tradition in correlation with their own personal, existential, and ethical experience, reciting the "acts of God" proclaimed in the Word, reflected upon by the church, and made present to us in the Spirit in the event of faith. They regarded theology as a discipline which necessarily for its own health remained completely autonomous in relation to the theories and implications of natural science.

Our point in describing this familiar twentieth-century understanding of the relation of religion and science as one of complete separation, is to dispute it as a self-delusion, and to try to show that some of the most important causes of the decline of the neo-orthodox view of religious truth stem precisely from this, its own distorted view of its relations to science. For the fact is that while (with the exception of the renegades Bultmann and Tillich) the neo-orthodox did not, as the liberals had done, deliberately or consciously refashion the Biblical Word to fit into the scientific world view they themselves accepted, nevertheless in their theological work they all presupposed important aspects of this modern view of things. Despite their protests to the contrary when they discussed hermeneutical *theory*, still the scientific world they lived in massively influenced their hermeneutic in actual *practice*. The theology that was ostensibly constructed solely on the Bible was in actual fact built upon and around certain basic assumptions of modern science and reflected in all its aspects this grounding in the modern scientific world view, though this dependence was never admitted and often denied. In much the same way one might build a house on some great rock, hidden by the house, but still determining its structure and shape, and making it very different from a house built in another kind of place.

As we have just seen, the first implication for religious language in the modern scientific world view was that religious language contains no factual information, since it does not contain indicative or informative statements about matters of fact, space-time events, nor is it concerned with the problem of the elucidation of the patterns of secondary causality. This implication of developments in modern science was assumed by all Biblical theologians as a basic if unexpressed hermeneutical principle in their search for, and interpretation of, the truth of the Bible and so of valid religious truth. They all took for granted that such questions as what had happened in the long story of cosmic development, of the gradual formation of the earth, of the aeons of developing natural life, and finally of the origin and development of mankind, and when and how these events had happened, were questions answerable only by the form of science appropriate to that field, and not by some further study, however novel or profound, of Genesis. In fact, to them, as they repeatedly insisted, *this* sort of information was not the real meaning or truth of Genesis at all, and they tended somewhat frantically to deny any interest on the part of the Hebrews in nature!

Whatever they may have meant, moreover, by "God's mighty acts," the neo-orthodox did *not* mean what the catastrophic geologists had meant, namely actual interruptions into the causal structures of the world process investigated by science, told to us by the words of scripture, thus uncovered, apparently, by the more energetic and brilliant of Old Testament scholars—and presumably phoned in at once to the astrophysics, the geology, and the biology departments of the university! None of them were in the slightest interested in Velikovsky's[34] attempt to show that the Biblical account of the stopping of the sun was in fact an accurate report of an actual cosmic event; and all of them were as unhappy as the most unrepentant atheist when, at Cecil B. DeMille's representation of the Exodus event, they found themselves gazing at a real pillar of fire, and staring through the walls of water at the fish!

Thus, however "Biblical" they tried to be, the acceptance

by neo-orthodox theologians of the modern scientific world view forced on them a new form of hermeneutic and as a consequence a radical transformation of their understanding of the whole Biblical story from Adam right through to eschatology. And what is noteworthy is that the way they told that refashioned story revealed their acceptance of scientific truth in every sentence.

In general, the story was retold on the following principles: God had acted, yes; but no longer had he acted upon the observable surface of nature-history. Rather, his activity was an "incognito," an activity related, to be sure, in *some* manner to the observable events of space-time, but *seen* as God's activity only by the eyes of faith, since to the ordinary observer all this would have looked like ordinary events, like, in fact, the world pictured by naturalistic scientific and historical inquiry.[35] *Heilsgeschichte*, the activity of God in the process, would not have been objectively observable had we been there to view it, as surely it would have been to the early nineteenth-century mind when the scriptural Flood was regarded as really and factually *wet*, as an event which could cause and so could explain the widespread distribution of the very real, observable, and often weighty, fossils! Nor was God's activity even describable in the terms of evolutionary theories of development which the biologists and the historians were wont to use, as in nineteenth-century liberalism. That activity was "there," and "real," but it was to be seen only by faith. Where that "there" was, if it was *not* in observable natural or human history, and still more *not* in some Greek eternity, was thus left a problem which has hounded Biblical theology almost to its death. In any case, our point is that one of the basic hermeneutical presuppositions of modern Biblical theology was itself not Biblical. On the contrary, it had its sources in the nineteenth-century history of the altercations of science and religion, which forced theologians and Biblical scholars to admit that religious language, and therefore Biblical language, does not entail any affirmation of matters of fact.

The second working presupposition of Biblical theology was derived from nineteenth-century *historical* science, though it was also the clear implication of the rapid changes scientific technology had been bringing about. This was a sense of the historical embeddedness of man and of all his works—be they his myths, his scriptures, his ideas, his philosophies, his theologies, or his creeds and his institutions. All are human products historically produced, shaped by the forces and attitudes that were there before them, and by those that are around them. Thus are all the products of history relative to their own time, and consequently strange and even irrelevant to another age. This historical attitude toward particular documents, ideas, and institutions had, of course, been applied to scripture and to historical theology by liberalism. Again it was one of the ironies of intellectual history that also this truth, learned by the liberals from modern science and historical inquiry, was regarded by the neo-orthodox, who inherited it in turn from their liberal fathers, as itself a part of the *Biblical* view they had themselves recently discovered! "The Biblical view," said the theologians, is that man is man and hence historical, his works are fragmentary, and even his theological truths relative and thus potentially swallowed up by passage—a view that would have made most former exegetes, especially Luther and Calvin, choke.[36]

The ultimate effect of this relativistic attitude toward all things historical was that no absolute authority for religious truth could henceforth appear in history in *concrete* embodiment: no document, creed, institution, or person could from now on have an absolute, changeless, divine authority. All available words and texts are relative: in scripture there is a

Yahwehist theme, a Deuteronomic view, a Lucan interpretation, a Pauline strand, and a Johannine tradition—and for us
now, of course, the redactors' imprint. Thus there are innumerable "Biblical" views, even more Christologies, and enough
eschatological viewpoints to match the passing years, all of
them relative, human witnesses to an event of revelation
which must thus lie quite beyond them. And as for ecclesias-
tical authorities: Does any canon law now transcend its
medieval, ascetic origins; can any body called the Curia now
rule with anything but Italian—and *old* Italian at that—ac-
cents; can any Pope seek to have influence except by per-
suasion?

Protestants smile at the anguished cries of their Catholic
friends, newly plunged into the icy waters of historical relativity.[37] They should reflect that they too are in the same
dangerous seas, and that their present indifference to this
fact may be because on the third time down you are too numb
to care!

In any case, the basic present problems for religious language and so for religious authority come from these two
notions developed in the nineteenth century, notions inspired
largely by the secular work of scientific inquiry into the past.
First, the sense that cosmic and historical process is an interrelated system of natural events elevated the divine activity
out of the phenomenal realm into that of the transhistorical,
of the "purely mythical"; and secondly, the sense of the relativity of all historical events and products relativized every
scriptural or theological proposition into a human and so
fallible witness to these elusive tranhistorical events.[38] Both
the *divine events* to which the Word witnessed, and the *Word*
in scripture which made the witness, seemed to have evap-
orated away in the naturalistic modern world in which the
theologian lived.

No wonder neo-orthodoxy has had subsequent problems in

our day with the status and the meaning of its religious truth and with its language about God! For it sought to locate religious truth precisely in what was thus evaporating, in the mighty acts of God witnessed to by a transcendently authoritative Word of God in scripture. But what were these "divine events" if they were understood neither scientifically nor metaphysically—and so if their referents seemed to be neither in history nor in eternity? And now with the relativization of all documents, what could be the authority of these "Biblical truths" if the scripture in which they were found was itself merely a collection of human witnesses? Biblical theology had located the source of religious truth unequivocally in the Word of God, in the Biblical Gospel, and in no sense in general human experience, historical inquiry, or the scientific study of nature. But that Word in scripture was increasingly hard to find and state with an authority and a precision commensurate with its ultimate theological significance. It was not identical with the relative words, concepts, or themes of the Bible, for these were human, relative, and fallible, and pointed to a hidden event behind them; nor was it to be found objectively in the discernible history of Israel or in the historical Jesus; nor was it evident in the history of nature.

As a result, most Biblical theology had inevitably but unwillingly to retreat inward to personal, existential experience to find the divine Word on which to ground its language.[39] It was only in God's Word speaking to me *through* these media in the personal, self-validating encounter of faith that God and his acts are known, understood, or spoken about—but was this not to be back again with Schleiermacher's location of religious authority in religious *experience*?[40] Neo-orthodoxy denied over and over that it located religious truth in subjective religious experience. Each time it tried, however, to find some objective locus for that truth, either in nature, in history, or in the words of scripture, its own scientific presuppositions condemned that very effort and drove it inward again. It was the assumed world view of modern science picturing events as a nexus of finite causes, and picturing man as embedded in historical relativism, that made finally unintelligible the objective, Biblical, and even theological language about divine events and mighty acts on which neo-orthodoxy had sought to build its theological house.

Neo-orthodoxy did not question the scientific picture of man in nature and in history, in the space-time world, as a creature embedded within a system of natural and historical causes and factors. There was no choice here for them since all of them went to doctors, drove Chevrolets, and tried in a friendly way to get along at the faculty club or the PTA with their scientific colleagues. In effect, therefore, the Biblical theologians accepted but then *desacralized* or *demythologized* that scientific picture of an evolving universe, and tried to keep it separate from their theology. They accepted science and its implications *secularly*, and thought they could go on doing their theological business precisely as the Reformers had done before the scientific age.

Thus they sought to build an autonomous structure of Biblical religious truth unrelated to their own scientific world view. What they were unaware of was that in the dark of night that world view of science, which they accepted, had radically changed their own hermeneutic, that is, the meaning, logic, structure, and authority of their own Biblical language about God's activity in the world. For these two worlds of *Heilsgeschichte* and *Historie*, and their appropriate languages, were impossible to keep apart, especially since according to the Biblical view God did enter into nature and into history. And each time the two worlds came together in God's "mighty acts," the scientific assumptions held by these modern theologians threatened the meaning and the authority of the Biblical Word that they also wished to affirm for our time. As nineteenth-century science had demolished an older orthodox view of religious truth which had provided "information" about specific space-time events in nature and in man's history, so the influence of twentieth-century science has likewise made unintelligible a neo-orthodox form of religious truth which sought, not to preempt the place of science, but to isolate itself completely from the influence of science.

The science of the past two centuries has seemed, therefore, to have had a twofold and somewhat discouraging message for religion and its truths: you can, it has appeared to say, neither be a part of us and be *valid*, nor separate from us and maintain any *meaning*. And as for the third mediating alternative, metaphysics, in which the two languages might be joined, who in our day feels he is easily able to do metaphysics? Apparently almost no one. Whether he be scientist, theologian, or strangest of all, philosopher, few modern thinkers have believed that what the metaphysician does is possible, or, even worse, is relevant for his work. The same history has apparently had many of the same effects on metaphysical knowledge as it has had on theology. This by no means establishes the death or even the uselessness of metaphysics. It merely means, as we have argued elsewhere, that a metaphysical inquiry suffering from the same disease can hardly be counted on to effect a rescue of theological language.[41]

This situation for religious language—of being unable either to associate with or to be separate from science—leaves us in our day wondering where theology is to go and what it is to do in a scientific culture. If indeed it be true, as our brief study has seemed to indicate, that the old warfare between science and religion is over, this *may* merely be because the total extermination of the religious opponent has already been accomplished![42] In the next chapters we shall seek to explore further, and hopefully with more positive results, the question of the place of religion and of theological truth in a scientific age.

II. Religious Dimensions in Science

IN OUR FIRST CHAPTER we traced the massive influence modern science has had on our current understanding of religious truth. We saw how in the nineteenth century scientific hypotheses had first of all quite banished religious categories of explanation from the field of spatiotemporal events. This in turn forced the total reinterpretation of religious or theological truth in a new direction, namely as entirely symbolic truth asserting something, to be sure, about the real, but nonetheless nonassertive of matters of fact, of events in space-time—which area was now left entirely to the inquiries of natural science and of history. And we then made the point that this exile from spatiotemporal matters rendered it difficult if not impossible for twentieth-century Biblical theology to maintain an autonomous Biblical language as the foundation of theological discourse. In short, it attempted to expound a theology *only* of the Word, and so a set of symbols seemingly quite unrelated to the world described by science and history. The result was that, as recent criticism has made clear, these purely theological systems of Biblical theology ended up empty, unreal, and meaningless. It seemed at the end as if religious language were thus excluded from a scientific culture, since its symbols have no place *within* scientific hypotheses, nor do they have meaning when separated off and raised *above* the scientific enterprise. In these next two chapters I wish to propose some other ways of looking at religious discourse within a scientific culture, and to show in the first how it has a ground even in the most "secular" of our pursuits, namely scientific inquiry itself, and in the next some of its important uses for a scientific society as it faces its future.

Let us begin by noting that the problems we have found science raising for contemporary theology are the same as those which form the center of the recent debate about the possibility of God-language. As we all know, this controversy about the death of God and the meaningfulness of God-language has arisen in large part because of the "secular" character of our culture. The essence of that secularity, we would suggest, is the rejection of a meaningful dimension of ultimacy or of transcendence either in experience or in the language that meaningfully thematizes our experience.[1]

Now the point is that it is largely, but not totally, a result of modern science and its implications that this secular mood has come so clearly to dominate all of our attitudes toward reality, truth, and value. As we saw in our brief historical survey, organized empirical inquiry (science in the broadest sense) has shown itself able to give us verifiable and useful knowledge of the significant factors operative in all classes of natural and historical events. It seems, therefore, to reveal, better than any other mode of knowing, what is both real and true in existence. And through its control over our environment and even ourselves, it seems to promise to man through the exercise of his intelligence and his moral sense an undreamed-of ability to enact his best purposes and achieve his most treasured values. If, then, the secular spirit can be defined as an attitude that sees reality as a system of contingent and relative natural or historical causes, to be understood by scientific inquiry, and to be manipulated by critical intelligence and political good will—if, in other words, it views the real as exhaustively defined by the contingent and the relative, and man's hopes as based exclusively on his own autonomous powers (and this *is*, I believe, what we mean by modern secularity)—then we can see how important the progress of empirical science has been in the development of this cultural mood.

It is equally obvious, moreover, that it is precisely this "this-worldly" mood that has created most of the difficulties for theological language which have exploded around us in the present crises of theology. If to our modern minds the real is confined to the contingent and relative factors traceable by science, if *all* meaningful and true assertions must be verifiable by scientific inquiry, and if our values lie here, solely in the industrial, communal, artistic, political, and personal creations of our autonomous powers, then we may well ask: What is real or even significant about God? What can religious discourse refer to or even mean? and Of what use are religious convictions, practices, and standards? At least, if the response of laymen, clerics, and seminary students to the radical theology is any guide, these questions about the meaningfulness and the use of language about God, the language of religion, represent the central issues that face theology today. To tackle them we must, I believe, enter into the inmost sanctum of this secular culture, namely its justified confidence in scientific inquiry and its optimism about the application of scientific knowledge to man's problems, and find *there* the grounds and the uses for religious discourse. This is what we propose to do in this and the next chapters.

In searching out the religious dimensions of science, we shall not follow one heretofore well-worn path. This is to base religious or theological notions or doctrines directly on the implications of scientific theories, that is, to regard scientific inquiry as a useful mode for establishing religious beliefs, and the theological task that of translating scientific theories into analogous religious notions.

We have seen that this enterprise was not uncommon during the nineteenth century, when the biological hypothesis of evolution was regarded as guaranteeing directly a cosmic law of development which might be called God. Although, as we noted, such forms of religious thinking are much less common today, still they do appear, and among some of our most distinguished contemporaries: Julian Huxley and many of the scientists in the Star Island group, on the one side, and Père Teilhard de Chardin on the other.[2] In each case scientific inquiry into the evolutionary course of nature is taken, as it is certainly by Huxley, as providing answers to the speculative religious or theological questions of man's ultimate origins, his destiny, and even his duties in relation to that destiny. Thus, as Huxley concludes,[3] because scientific inquiry has in its discovery of Evolution answered these age-old questions that man has raised about his destiny and obligations, there is no further need for religious truth or language over and above that of science. Science in itself has theological implications and thus replaces religion. If in orthodoxy religious concepts sought to do a scientific job, here scientific concepts, in answering our questions about destiny, claim to do all that religion, based on ignorance, once did. Thus can we rescue religion in a secular age and put it on a firm "scientific" basis of certainty and meaningfulness.

The difficulty with this view of the relation of science and religious truth, as Stephen Toulmin has brilliantly argued,[4] is that when scientific hypotheses are used directly to answer religious questions, they cease insofar to retain their function and status as scientific theories. As an answer to questions of ultimate origins and destiny, the concept of Evolution, Toulmin claims, is a "myth," a scientific myth to be sure, but surely no longer a precise theory in biology. Rather, it is now doing what all myths have always done, namely to provide that widest framework of understanding which underlies man's self-understanding, his activities, values, and hopes, and about which therefore he can never be precise or scientific. Such scientific myths are no longer science for a series of reasons: first, because their fundamental terms, for example, evolution, have been extended to cover phenomena their scientific use was not designed to explicate; secondly, because their function is now to answer questions quite different from the limited contextual questions of biology; thirdly, because they have thus lost their scientific precision and meaning; fourthly, because they are no longer verifiable or even falsifiable in their original scientific context; and thus, finally, in doing a vastly different "job" than they did in science, these terms have joined a different language game, and consequently have ceased to be scientific terms at all.

A theology based on science is still, even if its proposer be a scientist and its language made up of scientific terms, *theology* and not science. In seeking to answer questions about the ultimate issues of human destiny, it has itself become a proposal within religious discourse, a myth among other myths. It faces, therefore, not only the risk of the meaninglessness of all such discourse in a secular age, but, if it is to be defended at all, it must defend itself according to the criteria of the metaphysical and theological disciplines in which it now operates, and not those of science. Every culture must, says Toulmin, explicate symbolically these limiting questions; it must produce myths if it would live, and in a scientific age it is natural that scientific experience should become the basis of our own myths. These myths are, then, immensely significant, but as myths they no longer possess either the same meaning or the same certainty they possessed as scientific notions.[5]

The implication of all this is, therefore, that science cannot rescue religion in a secular age by lending out to a religion based on scientific theories its own prestige, certainty, and meaningfulness. For this is precisely what cannot be "lent out" beyond the range of science. Insofar as Teilhard de Chardin's magnificent vision claims to be science, it falls under the same criticism and is accordingly weakened. Insofar, however, as its inspiration, many of its sources, and much of its categorial structure stem forthrightly, as I believe they do, from his Catholic faith and from the vision about the whole of things and the certainty that that faith gave to him, his thought is an impressive and helpful *mystical* and *theological* interpretation of the data of science and history, and thus, in making no claim to the certainty and meaning of scientific hypotheses, it quite escapes this criticism. But by the same token, if this thought about the cosmos is based on a mystical vision and so enjoys a religious foundation, it can hardly initiate a scientific rescue of theology in a secular age!

If, then, we are not looking for theological elements in the *conclusions* of science, or even in the implications of special scientific theories, where *are* we to look? Our proposal is that we look in the activity of scientific inquiry itself. There, I believe, as in any expression of human autonomy and creativity, elements of ultimacy or of the unconditioned appear as the background and presupposition of what is done. It is these elements, the experience of the ultimacy involved in the knowing process itself, which pro-

vide one of the major secular bases for religious discourse—
even in the midst of the most secular of our enterprises, the
enterprise of science. The activity of knowing, like any
major cultural activity, points beyond itself to a ground of
ultimacy which its own forms of discourse cannot usefully
thematize, and for which religious symbolization is alone
adequate. These remarks about science as a human activity,
as will be obvious, are based on many wiser heads than my
own: on historians of science such as Charles Gillispie, John
C. Greene, and Thomas Kuhn, on a student of the language
of science such as Stephen Toulmin, on such philosophers of
science as Michael Polanyi and Bernard Lonergan, and finally on the philosophical-theological work in this field of
Karl Rahner and Paul Tillich.[6]

Each of these men, in his own way, has challenged the
traditional naturalistic account of science as an impersonal
activity based on a cool, tentative, logical intellect alone,
drawing inductions by rules from given data, to form theories or hypotheses which can then be objectively tested by
experience. If science be in fact such an impersonal activity
of a disembodied, uncommitted intellect, the only relevant
questions about this method are of course logical questions,
and a complete understanding of science is thus achieved
when the logical structure of its method, the status of its
theoretical terms, and the logical meanings of such acts as
verification or falsification are expounded. Such a view of
science as the imposition of an impersonal method on the
given data of experience, and therefore to be characterized
only by its logical structure and implications, is, to be sure,
still widely held today;[7] if it be accurate, then there are,
needless to say, few *theological* elements in science.

One might also add that there are few *human* elements
there. Science so understood seems less a creative act of
human autonomy than the automated act of logical ma-

chines. Ironically, science, which has been that aspect of modern culture which historically has most evidenced the power and vigor of human autonomy over against the imposition of supernatural authorities, has in our latter scientific day tended to be understood so as almost completely to dissolve again these human elements in favor of an impersonal logical system of inference, deduction, and verification. If the human act of creativity involved in knowing was once lost in a supernaturalist framework, it is no less currently obscured when scientific method is interpreted in purely objectivist terms as merely a mixture of objective experience and an objective logic.

These remarks by no means intend to deny that there are significant logical problems involved in scientific inquiry. We are only questioning whether a comprehension of these structures of logical interrelations constitutes *all* that is relevant to say about science as a mode of human knowing and an aspect of our cultural life—and so it is to these other elements that we shall now turn.

Incidentally, it might be added that when a theologian becomes discouraged by the inability of theology to give a reasoned defense or even a rationally articulated explication of the fundamental terms of religious faith, it is some relief to find that philosophers of science encounter the same inability, the same confusion, and the same disagreements when they seek to understand precisely what it is that is going on in scientific inquiry.[8] None of us concludes from this difficulty of articulating the theoretical structures of science that therefore science is either an irrational or a useless activity; nor in this case does it ever occur to us that a watertight articulation of the theoretical structures of science should be regarded as a test of the validity of the scientific enterprise. If our most rational of disciplines can hardly succeed in understanding its own procedures rationally, those of us involved in the understanding and intelligibility of religion may take some heart. If science be any sort of useful paradigm, possibly this shows that it is neither essential nor possible to articulate totally the foundations of our most significant activities.

The challenge to this impersonal view of science has arisen as a result of both a historical and a phenomenological analysis of science; we shall discuss the results of both. Recent students of the history of science have been impressed by the fact that apparently no logic of actual scientific discovery can be written. At each crucial change of fundamental framework in the history of modern science, a creative leap has occurred—what Polanyi calls a "logical gap" or Kuhn, more vividly, a revolution—which cannot be explained at all in terms of an impersonal application of the rules of induction. The reason is that what is in fact changed in such a revolution is the entire theoretical structure within which such rules are applied. Important scientific discovery and knowing thus take place outside the going logical system of any given science; it is, as Kuhn and Toulmin insist, a veritable "overthrow" of one order by another, a complete change in which every observable fact takes on a different aspect, old problems or questions now become irrelevant, and totally new problems, unguessed before, begin to dominate inquiry.[9]

If this is so, and the case that Kuhn and Toulmin advance is hard to reject on historical grounds, then the foundations of science must be reinterpreted. The impersonal application of a method—however it be logically understood and interpreted—is no longer an adequate description since apparently none of the important discoveries or advances of science have been achieved by the exercise of such a method. In fact, says Kuhn, the logical analysis of science is relevant as an analysis of the science that appears only *after* a new regime has taken over and "normal science" begins: when a new paradigm or ideal of natural order has established itself and scientific work consists in the application of this new theoretical framework to the wide spectrum of problems implied in its unfolding. At *this* point the impersonal application of induction, deduction, and verification makes sense as a description of scientific method. But this method itself presupposes the revolution establishing the new paradigm or theoretical structure in terms of which alone the problems, the relevant facts, and the significant experiments of any epoch of normal science arise as possible.[10]

The key theoretical point in this historical thesis, of course, is the insistence that in all scientific inquiry the investigation of nature or experience is "theory-laden." Relevant and important scientific facts are not just "there" to be encountered and generalizations automatically made from them. Rather, it is the fundamental theoretical structure already operative in the science in question that is creative of the problems which the scientist seeks to solve, that determines what are the "phenomena" or extraordinary facts given to him which he must investigate and explain, that defines counterinstances and anomalies, and that determines the character of the instruments he uses and of the experiments he finds rewarding.[11] There is no inductive movement from pure facts to a new fundamental theory, since each theoretical structure determines its relevant problems, its facts, and the methods of investigation. Objective inquiry takes place only within a presupposed framework— else it cannot take place at all. That framework itself is thus neither discovered nor sustained by the same objective inquiries it supports.

Furthermore, while anomalous facts can in the end render one of these basic theoretical structures shaky and dubious, apparently they cannot logically falsify it. No number of counterinstances or anomalies in the normal investigation of those puzzles involved in the application of fundamental theory generally seem able to disprove the theory; other elements of the theoretical structure can be brought in to explain the counterinstances, and, if this be difficult, they are left hanging as anomalies. Again, apparently objective inquiry can no more falsify than it can uncover or validate a fundamental theory.

What has happened historically, says Kuhn,[12] is that there gradually develops a crisis in the fundamental structure of the world view as a whole, as in Ptolemaic astronomy or in Newtonian mechanics, and then appears the "leap" to a new fundamental vision, illogical, unscientific, and even incredible in the light of the older view. To the mind of an Aristotle, Galileo's mechanics would have contradicted every relevant aspect of concrete experience and thus been without sense or reason; and Newton's idealized vision of inertial motion, which determined every problem and every significant fact for subsequent physics, would have seemed to any Hellenic or medieval inquirer sheer nonempirical fantasy unrelated to and so unsupported by all our experience of moving objects.[13] Scientific procedures and theoretical structures subsist within total world views or cosmologies which must be overthrown if a new *fundamental* scientific theory is to be accepted, explored, and enlarged.

The history of science, then, reveals that in actual practice science is based on creative leaps of imaginative vision. The heuristic process of knowing is, therefore, not founded merely on impersonal principles of inquiry and of validation applied to given facts, for at its inception each new view would merely be rejected by every current relevant mode of inquiry and of verification. Only those "converted" to the fundamental vision of a new point of view would allow as scientifically plausible the way the new vision poses questions and the problems it brings to light; only the "converted" would recognize the relevance and even the existence of its data, and regard its results as authoritative.

The most fundamental principles of science, therefore, are not based on objective proof; rather they are based on the convictions of those who hold them that *this* way of viewing things has relevance and fruitfulness. And even "fruitfulness" can be established objectively only *in the future*, through work accomplished in the slow inquiries of the normal science that results when the new vision has become orthodoxy. In itself, therefore, and at its inception the new vision is affirmed in risk and therefore in passion, and essentially it is *self*-validating, providing reasoned answers and valid tests apparent only to those who hold its general contours to be true.

Theologians and philosophers for some time have had to admit the inability of competing religious or metaphysical visions to prove themselves or disprove the others, and to recognize that their ultimate viewpoints are founded on conviction, on passion, and on the self-validating power of a fundamental vision of things to its holder. Philosophy, said Whitehead, is ultimately disclosure; its fundamental notions cannot be proved, for they are the basis of all relevant proof; we can in the end only say about a system presented to us, "Yes, that *is* the way things are."[14]

On its most fundamental levels, therefore, our intellectual life seems to be founded on a creative and autonomous act of human knowing. The *motivation* of this act is a concerned drive or urge on the part of our rational consciousness for the truth; the ground for *what* is affirmed is the self-validating grasp by that consciousness of what it judges to be true; and thus the ultimate *basis* for this act is inescapably our commitment in the midst of risks to a funda-

mental vision that may well be an error. Our most fundamental notions seem to be validated and validatable only
by the self-satisfaction of our intellectual powers, the self-
accrediting act of our rational consciousness that *these* notions, and not some others, reflect the way things actually
are. Knowing is thus through and through a *human* act, an
act of daring, commitment, and risk, a reaching for what
can never be incontrovertibly demonstrated, but which the
rational consciousness finds itself compelled on its own self-
accredited grounds to acknowledge and then to assert. Ironically, because it is a *rational* act and so autonomous, dependent on no external, necessitating authority but only on
the self-validation of the rational consciousness, cognition
is also an intensely *existential* or *willed* act, dependent on a
self-affirmation of the self as knower, and of the truth so
known as true—an affirmation that nothing else but the rational consciousness itself can finally establish. Interestingly, the history of science, surely the most methodical,
useful, and disinterested of the branches of human knowing, manifests many significant aspects of this character of
cognition as an act of rational passion, a personal act, as
clearly as do the others.

If the autonomy and personal character of scientific knowing is indicated in this way by its history, then let us proceed to investigate some of the structures implicit in this
account. What does knowing look like if we look at it not
as an impersonal application of a logical system but as a
creative and so personal human act? We shall, I believe,
find that this emphasis on the autonomous human character of scientific cognition leads surprisingly to an unveiling
of dimensions or contexts of ultimacy involved in knowing.
When man knows, as when he values, he makes contact with
something ultimate or unconditioned within and yet dis-

tinct from the relative and contingent character of what he knows.

As we recall, Augustine reasoned that in all acts of cognition, man's mind came into contact with something that transcends it, something eternal, absolute, unconditioned, and divine, which judged the mind and its knowing and so was not created by man's mind. This was Truth and so, argued Augustine, in relation to Truth in knowing, man was related to an absolute, eternal reality.[15] This Platonic analysis in its ancient form is not possible for us: in modern experience all truth is tentative, earthy, conditioned, and relative—we know no absolute truth anywhere, and do not expect to find any. Our question thus concerns the present validity of Augustine's view: What in the method and enterprise of modern science, as the process of human inquiry, is there, now translated into our contemporary modes of thought, that roughly corresponds to the absolute and unconditioned of which Augustine spoke? Does cognition, now as then, reveal a dimension of ultimacy in human experience?[16]

Let us begin with the most fundamental basis of scientific inquiry as a human enterprise, that urge, drive, or passion in man which it presupposes and so which makes it possible as a human act. This is the sense of wonder of which Aristotle spoke, the unremitting eros to know, the unrestricted passion of the rational consciousness to explain, to understand, and to judge validly—that lies back of all science as a human activity.[17] This is, as Tillich insisted, an ultimate concern, an ultimate commitment.[18] This concern in the scientist as he conducts his inquiry is the most fundamental of the prerequisites for knowledge. Without method, as the history of cognition shows, no knowledge is possible, but without passion no method is possible. For method demands *care*, a determination to know and so an unceasing dissatisfaction with not knowing; it thus requires also patience, rigor, self-discipline, and hope—and all of these presuppose a deep passion to know, cool and untemperamental as inquiry may seem from the outside.

Such passion or eros can take many forms, among them perhaps the following tonalities or commitments: whatever else I might wish, I will assent to nothing that is not established; I am not content to falsify or even to guess; I will accept no surrogate for understanding and verification; and I will continue relentlessly to ask questions, to probe, and to inquire until all the pertinent questions I can raise are answered—even if these questions render my own hypothesis more shaky than if I had desisted.[19] As is evident, there can be no relevant meaning to those standards of scientific disinterestedness and objectivity, which are essential to scientific inquiry, if the scientific community as a whole does not share this passion. And clearly, all scientific repugnance at prejudice, the closed mind, unexamined answers, and lack of rigor in facing uncomfortable truths, depends on this underlying eros to know.

Paradoxically, without such a passion to know superseding all other interests, a mind is not and cannot be "disinterested." For it cannot continue fearlessly to explore all anomalies and counterinstances and thus to expose even its own conclusions. And the very ability to hold truths important to the status and destiny of the self as tentative and relative is founded on the commitment to approximate more closely to the truth even at the cost of my own pet theories and so of my own reputation. Again, ironically, science as a human endeavor depends for its very achievement of objectivity and rationality on a deep, and in relation to other passions, an ultimate passion among the scientists to find and adhere to the truth.

Our culture has wrongly separated passion and commit-

ment from objectivity. This is one thing that the great John
Dewey understood with fine clarity; only, I believe, he did
not press far enough the phenomenological analysis of the
human concern that underlies inquiry. Some commitments
and passions, to be sure, do subvert the disinterested mind.
But in the welter of other pressures, personal and social,
science has been maintained only by the common passion
and commitment to the truth shared by the scientific community and passed on as a fundamental eros from master to
student as an essential part of his training.[20]

It is this passion to know that guides, as we have seen, the
isolated and often lonely creator of a new vision against all
the logic and experience of his contemporaries; it is this
that sustains arduous research into the implications of that
vision in normal scientific research; and it is this that makes
it possible for the community to maintain and transmit its
self-set standards, thus to be subject to fundamental revi-
sion of even its most firmly held orthodoxies, and so to continue the society of science in history. This is by no means
"faith" in the strictly religious and certainly not in the
Christian sense, and it would be quite wrong so to argue. But
it is a *commitment* in the sense that it is a personal act of
acceptance and affirmation of an ultimate in one's life, of the
good of knowing for its own sake, and thus of knowing
according to a set of undemonstrable but commonly shared
standards and aims, and it involves a quite undemonstrable
belief in the continuing rationality of experience. And finally
it is this commitment or belief that sustains the search for
an intelligibility not yet found but believed to be there—all
of this falling far short of any empirical or rational demonstration.

Such an affirmation is, for those who share it, necessarily
unconditioned. It involves, if we may put it this way, an
affirmation of the reality and value of the Logos in concrete

existence: the reality of a rationality characterizing that which is to be known, and so which is there to be found even if I have not and cannot demonstrate its existence; and a commitment to the ultimate value of that search and that achievement. Whitehead once remarked that the hope of rationalism is "that we fail to find in experience any elements intrinsically incapable of exhibition as examples of general theory"—and this faith "forms the motive for the pursuit of all sciences alike."[21] And we would add, science is equally dependent on the passion with which the mind and will of the scientist himself cleaves to that sacral Logos which he affirms to be characteristic of the reality to be investigated. In the sense that an ultimate (all-pervasive) and so sacred (ultimately worthful) order or rationality, cognitive union with which is truth, is presupposed in modern as well as ancient inquiry as traits of what is real, we may say we have found an aspect of a contemporary equivalent to Augustine's discovery of a divine truth embedded within our experience of ordinary truth.

The first element of ultimacy, then, that appears in the midst of the inquiries of the scientific community is the foundation of those inquiries in the shared *affirmation* that knowing is possible and in the shared *commitment* of this community to know, their personally held belief in the reality of order, and their passion for scientific integrity, their disdain for anything but the beauty, order, and simplicity of scientific explanation, and their refusal to affirm anything but what is veridically based on the evidence alone.

The second trace of ultimacy in scientific inquiry concerns not the commitments and beliefs which motivate it so much as the functioning of theories within it. Platonism was wrong in saying that all real understanding relates to truths which are absolute and changeless; but equally, modern theory has, it seems, made the opposite fallacy in feeling that *all* theoretical structures are held relatively in relation to the absolute authority of experience and of the data. For experience becomes intelligible only in relation to a given *method* of inquiry, and correspondingly the data are determined as relevant data only in relation to some presupposed *theory* about the data.

It is, as we noted, an "ideal of natural order," some "fixed set of laws or patterns" of nature's course, with which at any point in the history of science the scientist must begin. These paradigms, inherited from the recent past, create the kinds of problems he sees, guide his expectations, determine the character of his research experiments and instruments, and make sense out of the data he thus derives. Such theoretical constructs, such views of the way nature behaves and is to be understood, function as "absolutes" in the process of inquiry. As we have seen, they cannot be proved but themselves are or provide the basis of demonstration; they set problems and determine answers; and there is no argument between them. Apparently, just as a human cannot function importantly in valuing and in behavior without some form of ultimate commitment to some given set of values or other, so thinking and knowing cannot take place without some form of what we can only call a conditioned absolute. By this we mean some fundamental theoretical structure which is affirmed and believed to be true—since we cannot hold *this* in doubt and proceed in inquiry even to formulate and certainly not to test our own hypotheses at all. For it is in terms of such a theoretical structure, to which our science adheres at this juncture, that the welter of facts is so ordered as to be made manipulable, investigatable, and ultimately intelligible. As Toulmin remarks, "these ideals of natural order have something absolute about them."[22]

It has long been argued against the metaphysicians (for example, against Whitehead's claim referred to above), by the naturalistic and positivistic traditions, that a conscious metaphysical assumption of the uniformity of nature is not a necessary axiom for scientific inquiry or even for induction. This is probably true; the metaphysical presuppositions of science, as Polanyi says,[23] are never explicitly defended or even considered by themselves by the inquiring scientist. They arise as aspects of the *given* activity of inquiry, as its structurally implicit presuppositions, not as consciously held philosophical axioms preceding it. They are transcendental preconditions of methodical thinking, not explicit objects of such thinking; we think *with* them and not *of* them.

I would suggest on this point that it is probably true that a general ontological theory of the uniformity of nature is not consciously presupposed or possibly even logically entailed as an axiom by the scientist's operation. Nevertheless, as this analysis has shown, for any example of scientific inquiry to proceed at all, that is, for humans to conduct inquiry, they must, first of all, believe *something* of ontological generality about the character of reality as such and the relation of their minds to it—which belief can be explicated philosophically into an ontology and an epistemology. Some definite structuring of the most general context of interrelations—how things are related to each other and how intelligibility is related to being—must be assumed if we are to begin to understand objects in their relations to each other and to ourselves. Secondly, and this is our main point here, they must bring to experience not only this general metaphysical vision, but also some *concrete* view of natural order, some specific cosmology, some "ideal of natural order," if the mind is empirically to know its world. For there are no concrete problems, data, or relevant evidence without such a paradigmatic cosmology. In this sense a conditioned ultimate—some particular vision of the truth of things which is held to be itself nonrelative or hypothetical—is presupposed in all knowing. Here again, one aspect or trace of ultimacy is crucially present in the process of scientific knowing.

But how are basic hypotheses and laws confirmed, and these ultimate paradigms established, if, as we have seen, there is possible no automatic, that is, no logical or even empirical process of their verification or falsification on the most fundamental level? In answer to this question, many "objective" criteria have been suggested as useful in confirmation: for example, simplicity, generality, fruitfulness, elegance, and so on. While these represent, to be sure, genuine attributes of valid scientific theories, a careful analysis shows that they turn out to be discoverable attributes of theories which we *already* believe to be true or the fruitfulness of which normal science has long since illustrated, rather than criteria which can be objectively used to determine the validity of a new and as yet unestablished theory.

For example, as Polanyi notes,[24] the "simplest" explanation of Professor J. B. Rhine's data is that of extrasensory perception, but the "simplicity" and the "elegance" of this explanation would not be regarded as at all establishing its *truth* for most of the scientific community. And the reason is that that community holds a paradigm of natural order, a vision of how things relate to each other, that excludes the principles of such explanations (however simple and elegant they may be) as Professor Rhine offers. Thus such general rules or criteria are not in fact the criteria with which we actually discriminate between views of natural order, and so they do not tell us why we hold to be valid the most fundamental elements of our own theoretical structures. On the grounds of what objective criterion, for example, do most of the scientific community, and with them the naturalistic philosophers, assert the sole efficacy of *physical* causation in the explanation of all events? Ultimately, then, since objective rules or criteria do not explain the bases of our most important cognitive judgments, we must acknowledge that the most significant factors determinative of what we assert to be true or false are those ideals of natural order, and back of them that general view of the nature of things, which determine what for us are valid data and what for us is a useful method of inquiry. But as the bases of all inquiry and so of demonstration, such views of order ("of the relation of logic to reality," as Whitehead put it) cannot themselves be proved: they are not the results of inquiry but its presuppositions.

Thus it follows that these basic ground rules and criteria of knowing, the fundamental paradigms and models through which we think, are supported by personal affirmations of belief—or more probably, by the general affirmation of the cultural community in which we spiritually exist. If, then, our most fundamental judgments are not determined by objective rules, it follows that in the end they are, insofar as they are rational at all, determined by the self-affirmation of the rational consciousness alone as it is in our time and place historically understood, an affirmation in a self-accrediting act of insight that constitutes in each age the ground of fundamental judgment.[25]

Let us, then, next examine the structure of the act of judgment and see what this self-affirmation of the rational consciousness might be on which our knowing process is ultimately founded. As Bernard Lonergan insists, the eros of inquiry has a telos, a goal; it is intentional, directed at the end of understanding what *is*, of making contact through knowing with what is real, with what is *being*.[26] Its goal is not merely to conceive, to ponder, to produce possible explanations, or even to predict successfully. Its goal is to understand the real and thus it terminates in acts of judgment: "Yes, it is so," or "No, it is not so." The terminus of knowing is the enterprise of relating theory to fact, of verifying: we conceive in order to judge.

The act of judging is a strange one, in common sense or in science. First of all, a judgment is a personal commitment, an act of an autonomous, rational self-consciousness, something we do as a personal claim on ourselves, on reality, and on others. Although its intentionality is surely toward universality and utter objectivity, we make it *personally* as an affirmative act of our own centered self. It is, we feel, ours, for we know we are responsible for it: "We complain of our memory but not of our judgment," said de La Rochefoucauld.[27] It is personal, moreover, in the sense that not only *we* assert it, but also because it is self-accrediting. The criteria to which I subject my beliefs and judgments cannot themselves be demonstrated; they are ultimately upheld only by our own confidence in them as valid criteria.[28]

Without judgment there can be no science. There is no confirmation or falsification in any sense of hypotheses without judgment, for a judgment is what relates theory to fact, to reality. What, then, is the situation of making a judgment? A judgment of the rational consciousness with regard to a theory or hypothesis has conditions: if so-and-so turns out in fact to be the case, we say, then our theory seems correct; or perhaps we recognize it is only probable; or possibly it is neither and therefore is "false," as the case may be. A rational judgment about a theory is thus made when these conditions are seen to be fulfilled, when, as far as we can determine, no important questions are left outstanding which would render this judgment vulnerable, when, that is, the judgment is virtually now *unconditioned,* and therefore the proposition is and must be affirmed to be so.

It is at this point that the first element of ultimacy in judgment enters: when the satisfaction of the conditions is seen and so the proposition is seen to be virtually unconditioned. In judging at all that the relevant conditions are fulfilled and that "it is so," we experience the amazing possibility of finite truth in a universe the internal relations of which are infinite and so where qualifying conditions are endless. Scientific inquiry plunges into an infinity of mystery, symbolized by this infinity of qualifying conditions and further paralyzing questions. To be finite in the area of cognitive inquiry is to face this infinity and the corrosive doubt that nowhere is any utterly firm or demonstrable knowledge possible. The actuality of judgment thus bespeaks an experience of the overcoming of this infinity of conditioning qualifications—that now the proximate judgment is unconditioned and this finite truth can be affirmed.[29]

This experience is, or should be, a surprise and a wonder to us. For here the destructive relativity that threatens all finite judgments, endlessly qualified by unknown conditions, is overcome and broken by the achievement of even probable truths. However those presently unknown conditions may encroach back upon our frail judgment and render it improbable again instead of probable—and that we know will be its ultimate fate in the passage of time—nevertheless in making the judgment as now valid, we recognize that in fact the relevant conditions *are* fulfilled.[30] Thus the undoubted fact of judgments is evidence of the experience of the conquest of an ultimate relativity in which no finite truth could be possible at all. And this in turn indicates an apprehension that through our transient and relative experience of the fulfillment of these conditions, we have touched "what is" at some point, and made contact with what is not relative. That apprehension is, I believe, what communicates the "glow" to any glimpse of truth, and the peculiar excitement of discovery and of the brief experience of certainty in inquiry. Unless through our logical experience in cognitive inquiry of the virtually unconditioned character of our prospective judgments we relate to that which likewise transcends ultimate relativity in being, we could not say "it is so," and we could not have any sense that our inquiries had achieved *knowledge* at any point. The possibility of finite judgments amidst an actual infinity of unknown conditions by no means bespeaks our possession of absolute truth; but it does indicate that in making a finite and probable judgment, we ourselves have an apprehensive touch with, a prethematic sense or prehension of, something nonrelative latent within our cognitive grasp of what we judge to be so, and a necessary "transcendental condition" for our being able to know at all.

The second element of ultimacy follows immediately upon this prehension of the nonrelative. For our experience is that once having seen the unconditioned character of our judgment—that our theory "checks out" and that we can say "it is so"—*then* we cannot refuse to judge, nor can we remain in suspension. *What* is judged so, the content of the hypothesis, may be relative or probable; *that* it is to be judged so and that we must so judge it is itself an unconditional demand. In seeing, therefore, the unconditioned character of the judgment, we are compelled to affirm it. We do not then act as we *want*; we act as we *must*, that is, as rational beings. Our minds are bound by our own unconditional rational insight that the conditions have been fulfilled and that now, having seen this once and for all, we must not only assent to the validity of the judgment but lay the claim of this truth on ourselves and on others in the scientific community.

Rational judgment is to grasp the prospective judgment as now virtually unconditioned, to say, "Yes, by God, it is so," and to find oneself bound by this rational insight to what is there now known. Thus it is no longer possible for us to fiddle with the results; nor can we pretend that we have not made the judgment, that all is as it was before. We are bound now to the truth, as to something, as Augustine said, above our minds that determines and judges them.[31] This dual experience of ultimacy, of an ultimacy that transcends the relativity of all of our finite experience in an infinity of internal relations, and of an ultimacy that constrains our minds whether we will or not, must be presupposed in all our acts of verification or falsification if any human meaning is to be given to these two fundamental terms.

Furthermore, what precisely we cannot avoid in this situation of judgment, as any phenomenological analysis of an act of inquiry shows, is the knowledge that we now know. This knowledge that we know, this apprehension, whenever we make a judgment, of being related now to the truth, is grounded in an undeniable awareness of ourselves as now understanding and knowing whatever was to us a puzzle and unknown before. And our judgments following upon that consciousness—and the sequence from awareness to judgment is unavoidable—are grounded in an affirmation, made explicit in consciousness, then in speech, and so to the world, of ourselves as in this case understanding and knowing. What was in doubt before, has now been decided, and this experience is quite irreversible; we cannot pretend that we do not know what we now know, and know that we know. It is this irreversibility of cognitive time and our awareness of it, experienced in all scientific inquiry, that makes the cumulative march of science possible.

Fundamental to the proximate judgments that make up

science, therefore, is a still deeper unconditioned certainty and awareness than that which relates to the content of judgment, namely that in this situation I know myself with certainty as a knower. This self-awareness of myself as in this case a knower is the basis for the possibility of the cognitive judgment that "it is so," that the hypothesis in question—which is to become a part of the science of the future—was not falsified but possibly verified, and that we, and the scientific community with us, can go on from this new point to something else. This personal affirmation of oneself as a knower is, therefore, the foundation of the possibility of all rational judgment, and in the end it grounds all science. In turn this awareness of oneself as knower cannot be doubted. The skeptic, in affirming his skepticism, also is aware of himself and affirms himself as *understanding* the view that he now asserts; he is also aware of himself as *judging* conclusively that this view is in fact true.[32] As Augustine pointed out, the skeptic too knows that he knows.[33]

Most modern (as opposed to ancient) philosophers, for reasons that remain obscure, seem to regard only our acts of sensing as unconditionally trustworthy. However, as this analysis has shown, in the very heart of the act of knowing and so of inquiry, in the acts, that is, of understanding and of judgment, there appears another and firmer foundation of personal certainty on the part of our rational consciousness which also necessarily has an unconditioned character. Our rational consciousness sees the judgment as virtually unconditioned, and on the basis of that insight we can and do assert this as a claim on ourselves and on others because here we know that we know. Our knowledge that the conditions are satisfied, that the hypothesis fits the facts, that it is so, is one element in this unconditioned certainty of judgment; here we apprehend that amidst the infinite relativity of conditions, *this* at least is so, that in some way this judgment is unconditional and thus can be affirmed, that corroding doubt has been swept away. The other is that we are aware that we now know in this case. As the foundation of all our cognition, this knowledge that we know rests on a direct and unconditioned certainty.

No movement in science could take place without this element of indubitable certainty, without this unconditioned assertion of the actuality of knowing in ourselves. The unconditioned elements here are not by any means totally or in all respects absolute: our hypotheses may be merely probable, and we know this in making our judgments about them. But our judgments concerning them are virtually unconditioned: not that what we affirm is *necessarily* so, but that we must and do assert that it *is* so because the conditions are fulfilled.[34] And basic to this is the greater certainty of our self-affirmation as a knower: I know that I know when I judge—and on that bedrock of approximate certainty the whole human enterprise of inquiry has been built.

One might say that even within the contingency and tentativeness of the content of our judgments, there lurk elements of ultimacy as their possibility: the insight into the virtually unconditioned character of our prospective judgment, and the certain knowledge that in seeing this we really do know. It is this sense, fleeting as it is for us, of an unconditioned certainty that makes possible the relative and sharable certainties we do have, and so the communal and cumulative character of inquiry—that hypotheses are falsified and discarded, and a new vision established. All cannot be relative and tentative in inquiry: else we would never judge this to be the case, nor could we discriminate among hypotheses, nor be certain that such discrimination was ever valid. The process of inquiry cannot move forward unless it steps somewhere on firm ground, and that ground is the virtually unconditioned character of contingent judgments and our unconditioned affirmation therein of ourselves as knowers.

We have, then, looked into the human act of scientific inquiry and found there elements or traces of ultimacy: in the eros or passion that supports its individual and its social embodiments, in the role of global visions and of the theoretical structures that follow from them, and finally in the self-affirmation of the rational consciousness as knowing veridically in proximate judgments. These are the *human* aspects of science, what makes it a magnificent and creative product of man's rational autonomy—and yet they witness to a dimension of ultimacy, a relation to an unconditioned value, order, certainty, and being beyond our own making. They appear, as we have seen, in strangely conditioned forms: as if, as Paul Ricoeur has said, man were even in knowing a strange mixture of the conditioned and the unconditioned, of the finite and the infinite.[35] Nor do we mean to imply that with this dimension of ultimacy we have so easily uncovered "God"; nothing we have said so far would as yet legitimize the application of that symbol. That even this most creative of the aspects of our secular culture, however, is grounded beyond itself in a dimension of ultimacy, which only a symbolic language appropriate to that dimension can thematize—*that* we have tried to show.

If, then, we ask, where on earth in a secular culture do those regions of experience appear with which religious discourse deals, and to what sort of real problems do religious symbols usefully relate, surely we now have the beginnings of one answer. Religious language and its symbols have one of their secular foundations in the tacit experience of ultimacy revealed in the passions, the theoretical structures, and the rational judgments of science itself.

Finally, we may ask: Why is the uncovering of these pre-suppositions or preconditions of knowing a matter for theology, and their thematization a matter for religious or mythical discourse? Is not this the classic role, or one of them, of philosophy—and therefore as secular as is science itself? Granting that transcendental philosophy has legitimate rights in this area—for one of the strange roles of philosophy as a mode of knowing is to wonder about its own grounds—let me conclude by saying why I think inevitably one is led to mythical or religious discourse when one approaches this sort of question.

In the first place, the grounds of knowing inevitably transcend knowing itself, and so they transcend even the most foundational of all its forms, namely philosophy and its language. One may couch this aspect of transcendence in the idealistic language of a principle of identity between thought and being, a principle which itself cannot be explicated rationally; or may explicate it in the coy mythology of Santayana as "animal faith"; in Heidegger's heavier mythology, that Being speaks to and in us when we know; or in Whitehead's more precise statement that there is a basic faith in the rationality of things that guides all knowing, hence all philosophy itself. Whatever phrases one uses, inescapably since we are dealing with the foundations, the presuppositions of knowing, our language transcends even the philosophic discourse which is thus grounded, and our language penetrates into a deeper region of mystery, where affirmation and assertions are based more on deep intuitions and on faith than on argument—since we are dealing with the foundations of all argument.[36]

Secondly, as our analysis of these grounds of knowing has shown, here we reach not only into mystery and therefore beyond ordinary, univocal chains of reason; more than that, we are dealing with a level of ultimacy. For at each point when we uncovered a foundation of knowing, we met not simply something, anything, that lay below our cognitive capacities. Rather, we met an ultimacy, an aspect or trace of the unconditioned, a whiff, if you will, of the sacred, as the source and ground of this most human, rational, and "secular" of activities. Since, then, traditionally it has been mythical discourse that has dealt with the heights and depths of existence, and since, as Plato reminded us,[37] myth does this even more gracefully than can logos or abstract discourse, we may say we have uncovered one use for such language even in a secular culture.

III. The Uses of Myth
in a Scientific Culture

I N DISCUSSING THE USES OF MYTH in a scientific culture we presuppose, on the one hand, that our culture is
and will remain scientific in its predominant understanding
of knowledge, of reality, and of truth, and that its characteristic ways of dealing with problems will be in terms of
objective rational analysis leading to a technical resolution.[1]
On the other hand, we shall argue that even in such a culture, the peculiar language of myth and therefore of religion is not only necessary because unavoidable, but even
more it is essential if a scientific culture is to deal creatively
with its own peculiar problems and so its own destiny.

Thus does our picture of the interweaving of myth, science, and theology approach completion. We have shown
how scientific knowledge has acted to transform, possibly
to purify, the essential language of myth, and of the theology which is the disciplined reflection on the mythical symbols of a particular religious or cultural tradition. Next we
sought to uncover the dimension of ultimacy latent in cognitive inquiry itself, as it is latent in all significant human
activities, a dimension expressible only in the language we

have called mythical. And now we seek to show how in our understanding of the *uses* of scientific knowledge, and of the question of the *destiny* of a scientific culture, there is a creative and necessary usage of the mythical symbolism of religion.

If we are to show the important usage of mythical discourse in a scientific age, we must first define what we mean by mythical language with perhaps more precision than we have done heretofore. Clearly we shall not approach our subject, as do some anthropologists, on the assumption that because the myths of other cultures with which they are professionally familiar are apparently untrue by modern standards, all myths represent a primitive form of discourse irrelevant in that form to mature society.[2] Myths to us, then, are not just ancient and thus untrue fables; rather, they signify a certain perennial mode of language, whose elements are multivalent symbols, whose referent is in some strange way the transcendent or the sacred, and whose meanings concern the ultimate or existential issues of actual life and the questions of human and historical destiny.

Archaic mythical language, the language of ancient religious symbol systems,[3] was a form or type of language expressive of a certain mode of human self-understanding, namely one achieved through an experienced relation of intimacy to the fundamental sacral structures of man's cosmic environment. The symbols which composed such a mythical structure were, as we noted, multivalent in a special manner; they referred not only to a finite thing (sky, stone, spear, animal, person), but at once also to the transcendent, the unconditioned, and the sacred that appeared in and through that thing and was, therefore, in a variety of ways identified with it. Thus mythical language talked about *both* finite things and their relations, *and* the sacred or ultimate manifested in and through them. As we noted, this characteristic has been the source of most of the recent problems of mythical discourse in relation to scientific and historical knowledge.

Generally, moreover, ancient mythical discourse referred to the cosmic origins of finite things. Archaic myths were cosmogonic, that is to say, the sacred manifesting itself in and through the present symbols was identified with the *originating* divine power of things, of time, of space, and of natural and especially of social (tribal or national) forces. It followed, thirdly, from the cosmogonic character of most ancient myths, that human existence was believed to escape dissolution and disorder by repeating the original and founding forms of things. Whenever, therefore, these originating forces repeated themselves cyclically in time, there men might find renewal and freedom from disarray. Hence in ancient myths there was inevitably a backward look, a cyclical view of the sacred structure of time, and, finally, a sense that man's freedom was fulfilled, not in creating new forms of existence in future time—as in modern life—but only when men reenacted or repeated these religiously given, original forms posited into existence at the beginning by the gods. We may sum this up by saying that the traditional language of religious myths referred to the transcendent within the finite, was attentive to the cosmic origin of creaturely and social existence, and sought to model man's life on these original cosmic structures and exemplars.

Our next question in finding the role of this sort of language in a secular culture is: Why have these characteristic elements of mythical language been challenged if not exorcised in the modern secular age? Clearly this is a very complex question, involving almost every aspect of the intellectual development of modern man and of the secular spirit which characterizes our age. For our purposes, three elements of that spirit are relevant to the gradual waning of the intelligibility of mythical language:

1. Characteristically, the secular mind understands events in terms solely of the nexus of finite causes within which they take place. Thus explanation is confined to either the physical or the historical causes of the event, since it is only in these terms that scientific and historical inquiry can explain anything that occurs.[4] A "transcendent" or a "sacred" factor or structure present in and active in and through the finite is therefore unknown and unreal to this mind. All that is real and effective are the contingent and relative factors succeeding one another on a finite level. As a consequence there is no meaningful mystery beyond this level about which we must or even might speak if we are to understand either our environment, our history, or ourselves. Thus the multivalent character of religious symbolism to this mind has not been a mark of the uniqueness and significance of this type of language, but rather a sign of prescientific superstition, and of the inevitable error, emptiness, and unreality of mythical speech.[5]

2. Characteristically, therefore, the sacred has tended to vanish from the objective environment of man. The cosmos or nature no longer provides a sacral setting for man's life, giving to that life its intelligibility and its potential meaning.[6] A spiritual separation between man and his cosmic environment has occurred. That environment is for most of us characterized only by contingent, relative, and blind or purposeless factors. Thus to many, man is "on his own," utterly dependent on his own autonomous powers if there is to be any meaningful order or value at all in his life. Insofar as myth is comprehensible to most moderns, therefore, it represents the mistaken projection of the sacral potentialities of *man*'s creative powers or psychological history onto a desacralized outward cosmos.[7] We can understand religious myths, we say, if we can give them a Freudian or

Jungian explanation, or see them as projections of social hopes and frustrations onto the cosmos. Almost by second nature all of us—even those of us who recognize forms of religious authenticity—feel we *understand* why depressed people have believed so fervently in their religion's heaven, not when we regard the Biblical authority to which they appeal, but rather when we consider their social plight and the fact that they were so long barred from the rights and delights of earth.

The factors causative of this development of the alienation of modern man from his cosmos are many: the demise of all the gods of nature through the Biblical, Christian tradition; the radical continuation of this process in science since Galileo through the rigorous eradication of all teleology, valuation, and "meaning" from the processes of nature; the spiritual or existential separation of man from both the beauty and the awe of surrounding nature which technology and urbanization have gradually effected; and, finally, the gradual loss, culminating in the twentieth century, of a sense of an ultimate order or directedness in the process of things.[8]

3. Correspondingly, the modern spirit emphasizes the creativity of human autonomy, the possibility of the "new" in historical existence, and above all the dimension of time as the arena of human meaning. It is oriented not *backward* to an essential cosmic order in which man's freedom must participate, as were ancient cultures, but *forward* to a potential existence in the open historical future which man's freedom may create.[9] For this reason the mythical seems to our age to be not only prescientific and superstitious, not only empty or nonreferential and subjective, but also repressive and thus destructive, imprisoning man's autonomous and creative spirit in a predetermined cosmic niche, and setting essential limits to the freedom of man in history.

"God is dead" thus becomes a cry not only of rationality

and maturity, but also a slogan of freedom, of openness to the future, of history as opposed to nature.[10] Since in this phrase the symbol "God" connotes the whole range of the traditional mythical consciousness, it is not surprising that all those other relics of the mythical consciousness that have traditionally structured the spiritual existence of the West, and so have provided the foundations for its metaphysics, its moral philosophy, and its theology, have in our age accompanied the cosmic creator into his grave. These "relics" include the belief in the objective logos of existence that made rational metaphysical speculation possible, and made science itself intelligible; the sense of an "ought" standing over man's freedom which provided an inward locus for the moral experience of the sacred;[11] and the sense of a final goal toward which all process moves and which in the nineteenth and early twentieth centuries gave meaning to the teleological symbol of the divine providence.

The opposition between the modern spirit, informed by a scientific view of the cosmos and by a corresponding faith in man's absolute autonomy, and the traditional mythical consciousness in all its facets, seems, therefore, to be absolute. We suggest that a certainty of this absolute opposition between modernity and myth is itself one of the fundamental characteristics of the modern spirit. Mythical language having to do with the transcendent and the sacred is to much of the modern mind superstitious, nonsensical, and repressive, and the supposed referents of this language are unreal and unneeded in today's world. It is of the essence of the "geist" of secular modernity to believe that myth is part of the infancy of man, and except for its artistic, literary, and psychological values, is to be outgrown in a scientific and autonomous age.

We also suggest, however, that there is a split or a disjunction between modern man's *intellectual* comprehension of himself and his world—which we have called the modern spirit or mind—and his more *existential* self-understanding; that in fact the terms in which he explicitly thinks or talks about himself are different from the terms by which he actually lives. There are many evidences of this split between the secular attitude or viewpoint on the one hand and secular existence on the other, but certainly one of them is the continuation, or better, the re-creation, of myths within the modern consciousness itself. Strange as it sounds after the preceding discussion, there are modern secular myths as well as archaic and traditional myths. Naturally they take quite different forms than have the archaic, cosmogonic, or even the mythical language of our own Christian theological tradition. Consequently our concern now is to see (a) in what way they are myths and function as such in modern culture; and (b) how in the secular setting the mythical consciousness expresses itself and some of the problems it encounters there.

We have characterized the modern view as suspicious of any multivalent symbolism, any intelligibility beyond the one-dimensional sequence of contingent and relative factors that, to an empirical investigation, bring things about. Thus is the cosmos out of which man comes desacralized of meaning, and man's obligations and prospects alike understood solely in terms of the development over time of man's own inherent powers. What sort of myths are possible in this atmosphere?

First of all, it is not surprising that cosmogonic myths—myths referring to the sacred *origins* of things—would now be virtually unknown. Almost no modern understands himself or his world on this level in terms of its origins, or seeks to renew his life by returning to the original and divinely founded structures of space, time, nature, and human being, either individual or social. The question of origins has in fact moved quite out of the realm of sacral mystery and thus of myths, and has become a series of "problems" for the inquiries of the special sciences—astronomy, geology, biochemistry, biology, anthropology, etc. Such structures as are found at the beginnings have, therefore, no exemplar function for us.[12] Early man is, for example, an object of fascination for all of us, but it is not out of scientific views of the original structures of human life that our current scientific myths about man, his capacities and obligations, are fabricated.

Because of modern man's view that he exists primarily in time rather than in space, and that time is a process developing toward a goal rather than a medium for the cyclical repetition of eternal structures, modern man finds his locus of meaning in the patterns of *development* in time, and ultimately in the *goal* at the end of time, rather than in its originating structures. As an aside, it is thus not strange at all that much of the most "modern" theology is oriented eschatologically, toward the future end of time, and not toward either the sacral origins of being at the Creation or its eternal order in the Logos, and that correspondingly it finds the focus of theology to be *sociohistorical* rather than cosmological or ontological.[13] Modern man's models for his own existence thus typically arise out of a vision of *future* utopias rather than from the memory of lost or originating paradises.

Correspondingly, the sense of the creative powers of his own freedom: his freedom over his natural environment, over his given social institutions, over his own moral norms and decisions, and even over his own physical being, make modern man feel that original structures are merely "given," and that to appeal to them and their authority is to appeal to the as yet undeveloped and so to the insignificant. All they provide is *material* for our free, creative action, not forms to be copied by our freedom; man must create his own models for himself and not accept them passively from God, the cosmos, or even history.[14]

If cosmic origins and an eternal order are thus no longer relevant to man's self-understanding, does this imply that modern myths in no way express a union of man with the structures of a wider cosmic setting of his life? This does not follow, and in fact the two primary modern myths, by which the majority of men in our present secular world probably still actually live and find meaning, can, despite their orientation to history rather than to nature, be called global or "cosmic" myths. That is, they explicate a vision of the ultimate nature of reality or of process as a whole, and seek to understand man's nature, obligations, and destiny in the light of that total cosmic vision. What is "modern" about these cosmic myths is that they understand life in terms of the *historical goal* of a changing or developing process rather than in terms of the eternal, static structure of things manifested at their *cosmic origin*. These modern myths are, first, the liberal view of cosmic and historical Progress, well summed up in the great word Evolution, and, secondly, the allied but nonetheless significantly different vision of Marxism, with its belief in a Historical Dialectic that is moving inexorably toward the communist ideal. Both Cosmic Evolution and the Marxist-materialistic Dialect represent "myths" in our threefold sense.

1. As applied to the whole of process, they do not represent limited hypotheses within the range of a particular science and its modes of explanation. Rather, they deal with the universal structures and patterns of things, patterns which are thus hidden as well as manifest to the eye, and can neither be verified nor falsified by any particular scientific investigation. They must use multivalent language, speaking of universal and ultimate structures or powers

within the observable interrelations of things.[15] Thus they
are validated not by objective inquiry but by a deep intuition of the character of the whole of things, a vision based
on certain factual clues taken to be revelatory of that mystery, and so a vision upheld by involved participation in the
spiritual ethos and the ethical structures of the community
formed by the myth—as in the case of liberal Progress or
the Communist Dialectic.

2. They give an intelligible explanation of the evils and
enigmas of historical life and contain as well a vision of
an ultimate "purposive" structure determining the character of events. As religions have always done, therefore,
they provide "meaning" in life in that they are explanatory
of its evils and reassuring about its prospects. It is significant
of the religious or mythical character of both liberal hu-
manism and Marxism that in both of them normative or
"ought" language, what in the minds of the adherents of the
myth *should be*, becomes in the future tense identical with
indicative and assertive language about what *will be* the
case. According to each of those myths, the good and therefore the sacred will be embodied in the actuality of the future; hence it is correct to say that these modern myths,
however "scientific" their base, are eschatological in character.

3. They imply within their scope models and norms for
individual human existence, for social and political decisions, and for the patterns of education and social life characteristic of the cultures which live by them. No system
of scientific hypotheses functions in these three ways. Thus
the *meanings* of these visions are mythical and not scientific,
and whatever *validity* they possess is to be assessed for them
as myths and not as science.

Although these two cosmic myths retain an important
role among many of the more powerful elements of the

modern secular scene, it seems to me that since the early part of the century they have both tended to be replaced by anthropocentric myths, and that the latter are in the end more characteristic of our present secular culture. What has happened, apparently, is that the questioning, empirical, secular spirit has now begun to devour its own cosmic myths, to separate them as myths from their own scientific foundations, and to test them increasingly by the scientific and historical evidence at hand. For this reason evolution has more and more become a lower-case word, a theory in biology and the life sciences, and is no longer generally regarded, as it surely was at the end of the nineteenth century, as a universal law of cosmic and historical progress. Where mythical elements still linger around this concept, they do so in terms not of the objective course of evolution, but of man's newly developed ability to take evolution over and to direct it; that is to say, they lie not in what is called "natural evolution," but in what is, I think, somewhat confusedly called "cultural evolution."[16] And the Marxist ideology has become increasingly regarded by its adherents in Eastern Europe as a defensible theory applicable to economic and political life, but not an ultimate framework totally explanatory of man and his world.

The results of this further development of secularity, therefore, have been a deeper desacralizing of the cosmos and of historical process, a total separation of the great human questions of meaning and direction from questions about the nature of the universe and even of history as a whole, and hence a waning of what we have called "cosmic" mythology. Thus in most modern thought the cosmos is *merely* nature as understood by science, and history *only* what specialized historical research can uncover, namely systems of contingent, relative, and temporal factors illustrating no ultimate purpose or direction and therefore irrelevant to

human questions of meaning and to human hopes for a
better world. Man is here "come of age" in a directionless
world. His confidence about life and the models by which
he structures his freedom tend, therefore, to be reflective
not of any ultimate cosmic or historical structure, but only of
the capacities and achievements of his own autonomy. Most
postmodern myths are thus myths about man and his
powers.[17]

When in this context we speak of myths of human autonomy, we are speaking of images of man and his capacities
which carry with them a sacral character and can function
in our culture as myths have in other cultures. More spe-
cifically, this means that the language in which such myths
are described is multivalent or symbolic in form and thus involves assertions far transcendent to the level of empirical
or scientific discourse. It means as well that the narration of
the image answers our ultimate questions of destiny and of
meaning. And finally, it means that these images provide
models or norms for important social behavior. Thus the
lack of the cosmogonic or even of the cosmic and historical
referents, characteristic of previous mythologies, does not
vitiate the mythical character of much of modern discourse. It merely means that the sacred, that which is ultimate, healing, and normative for us, and that which gives
meaning to the chaos of our life, manifests itself in and
through man and not in and through the environing
world, its history, or its processes.

In such anthropocentric myths the "given," that which
is delivered to us from our cosmic or historical setting, is regarded as initially meaningless; only what man can make
of what is given to him can have meaning. It is no surprise,
therefore, but surely ironic in a naturalistic culture uncertain there is anything other than matter, that these secular
and so naturalistic myths are generally *gnostic* in form: the

sacred is precisely not matter but spirit, manifesting itself in and through the exercise of man's reason and will, rather than through the given of natural or historical process. Each form of modern anthropocentric myth—asserting that man becomes *man* and can control his life and destiny if he is educated, liberal, analyzed, scientific, an "expert," etc.— assumes that for man at last to understand, to know about, or to be aware of something—for him to have a sacral gnosis —is for him to be able in a quite new way to control that object of knowledge, to direct it, and to use it teleologically; that knowledge and awareness can turn whatever has been a blindly determining force *on* and *in* man, and so a fate *over* man, into a new instrument *of* man.[18] Or, in the language of modern life sciences, that a blind "natural" evolution can become a purposive and benevolent "cultural" evolution; or, in classical language, that knowledge gained by science and applied technologically as knowhow will provide at last human self-fulfillment or *arete*.

Correspondingly, such myths also share the confidence that the actualization of human freedom, however the latter may be defined, will mean freedom *from* evil rather than freedom *for* evil, and thus that in freeing man—from whatever is determining him against his will—awareness or knowledge (gnosis) at the same time resolves the problem of evil in his behavior and so the ambiguity of his history. In these myths, therefore, evil is located outside of knowledge and of freedom; insofar as man is really free to be his mature self—entirely educated, critical, authentic, unrepressed, liberal, or what have you—to that extent is he free from the evil that has haunted him. Fate and sin arise from beyond the inward center of man: in ignorance, in repression, in unawareness, in the false objectification of others and of himself as a thing, in prejudice, or in false ideals. Consequently, man may have confidence because the rapidly accumulating knowledge or awareness of man must lead to an increase of meaningful experience.

Surely one of the most important characteristics of a scientific, introverted, specialized, hence infinitely intellectual culture is its drive toward, and faith in, total "awareness." Awareness of almost every conceivable factor influencing almost every conceivable situation is our characteristic panacea or cure-all. In this sense, gnosis, total consciousness, and self-consciousness are the major goals of our secular culture. We really believe that if we know or are aware of everything, if we understand all relevant causes and factors, we can control everything. And the range of the "problems" to be so dealt with is infinite: traffic problems, air pollution, international war, causes of social alienation and crime, unrest and revolution, poverty and maldistribution, mass violence, our psychic disorders, even how to raise our children. This faith in the healing power of knowledge or awareness in a culture in which objective knowledge accumulates at an accelerated pace leads to a tremendous optimism about a new day, an eschatology in which an understanding of all the factors outside of us and a self-consciousness about all those within us will result in total control and thus healing enjoyment. In the typology of the myths of humanity generally, therefore, modern anthropocentric myths are dualistic accounts of destiny in which "evil" is a result of the chaos of the unorganized and so unintelligible given; but it is a "given" which the intelligence and good will of the trained, the self-aware, or the critically intelligent man may, like Indra or Zeus of old, subdue into order through a sacral gnosis and autonomous freedom.[19]

We cannot discuss in detail the problems of each one of the variations of the modern gnostic myths of autonomy, but we might spend the remainder of our time summariz-

ing the principal difficulties, as we see them, of that anthropocentric myth which, we feel, represents the dominant
source of confidence, reassurance, and meaning in the present West: the myth of the new scientific man. And then
we shall seek to show the greater relevance of the mythical
symbols of Christian discourse to the understanding of man,
his powers, problems, and destiny.

The myth of the new scientific or technological man presents to us the image of the man in the white coat; the man
who embodies the gnosis achieved by the new methods of
inquiry. This man thus in modest actuality but also—and
here is the first element of the mythical—in infinite potentiality *knows* the secrets of things, what their effective structures are, and therefore how they work. Consequently—and
here is the second mythical element—he is the man who
can control these forces which he now understands and
bring them into the service of human purposes. This control over the blind forces of our natural environment—so
the myth continues—has already been partly realized
through technology. Why cannot the same sort of knowing,
directed now at man's own psychological, social, and historical problems—yes, even at the genetic structures which
determine man's nature—lead to the same kind of control
over human life and thus lead at last to the directing of
our own biological and historical destiny along the lines of
human purposes? We are beginning to see that man can
now create not only a new environment, but also literally
a new man; and thus man can free himself from every aspect of his former bondage, from bondage both to the ex-
terior and to the interior forces that have worked against
his will.

Let me quote, as one among many examples—Julian
Huxley is probably the best known—from a recent speech
by the distinguished scientist Dr. Glenn Seaborg. As quoted

in the *New York Times* of January 17, 1963, in a speech in Washington, D.C., Dr. Seaborg "expressed faith that man could, if he tried, solve all of today's agonizing problems—war, hunger, the population explosion, water shortages, pollution. 'Man may well have reached that point in history, that stage in his development . . . where he has not only been made master of his fate, but where his technology and his morality have come face to face.' . . . Science has given mankind an opportunity 'to control and direct our future, our creative evolution. . . . I believe we can be masters of our fate.' "[20]

Modern academic, scientific, professional man does have confidence in the meaning and the vast possibilities of human life. If one asks about the ultimate grounds for that confidence, something like this myth will appear: we now know how to know; we have unlocked the secret of critical intelligence. With that sacral tool we can change the character of the natural environment that surrounds us, of the sociohistorical context in which we live, and even of our own weak, temporal, and recalcitrant nature. Thus can we master evolution and through it even history and destiny themselves.

Much might be said of this myth. The first relevant point is that like most myths it deals—whether it is aware of it or not—with the mystery of destiny and of human freedom. Arising as it does within a scientific context, however, this secular myth sharpens this ancient paradox into what is almost a self-contradiction; and this self-contradiction, without the explicit aid of the multivalent, symbolic language essential to myth, must remain unresolved, in fact self-contradictory. The image of the new scientific man able to understand and so able to control the determining forces of destiny is an image which promises a more extravagant freedom than has almost any previous mythical image—

even that of Prometheus. For, let us note, the irrational and purposeless forces of "fate," both natural *and* historical, both outside *and* inside man, are here felt to be, potentially at least, under the domination of man's rational and moral purposes. Decision or intentional choice are thus in prospect given an almost unlimited range over history and cosmos alike.

Linguistically, moreover, the same emphasis on an increase of freedom is undeniable. At the conclusion of most articles and books on man as understood by the new sciences, the issue of the responsible and creative *use* of our knowledge is pointedly raised over and over. The language in which this set of problems is discussed is what we can only call the traditional language of freedom. Every sentence stridently urging a moral, rational, and thus responsible use of scientific knowledge includes such key words as "responsible," "rational," "moral," "choice," "decisions," "purposes," etc.[21] When science therefore speaks of the application of knowledge, it seems to paint a quite different picture of man than does the voice of science as inquiry. Man here is seen as an initiating moral and rational *cause* as well as the determined *effect* of natural and historical forces—which is what the category of freedom has sought all along to say. To the cynical observer, it might almost seem that the category of freedom, if defended by theologians or philosophical existentialists, is inadmissible in a scientific age, but that the same category, voiced by the leaders of the scientific community, is thoroughly in tune with the aims and aspirations of that community.

Paradoxically, however, the hope for this vast increment of freedom through scientific knowledge depends directly on the assumption that for scientific inquiry—in genetics, biochemistry, neurology, psychology, and the social sciences —man himself can exhaustively be understood as the determined *object* of inquiry. Man is thus inescapably conceived as an object to be comprehended in terms of the necessitating universal factors or laws that operate in and through him, comprehended therefore precisely as a nonintentional creature, a part of nature's total system of determining factors, and as a being to whom the category of freedom is wholly inapplicable by those who know!

But if the man in the white coat is as free to control, and as intentionally motivated by creative and moral purposes, as the mythical image proclaims—and otherwise there is little hope in the image—then the man on the table, the object of the inquiry of the same scientist, must *also* be in part free. Thus man as a free being, the object of inquiry, must in part be *in*comprehensible in terms of objective and universal laws, and even creative outside the bounds of those laws, and consequently potentially destructive of them as well. Any freedom in the object under control reduces inevitably the freedom of the controller to work his will. As Tillich was wisely wont to remark: man can always look back at his controller—and, we lesser mortals might add, cheat on an objective test. And so, since in this case both controller and controlled represent instances of the same sort of being, this myth about man tends to contradict itself. A myth which promises to man freedom *over* necessitating destiny on the basis of man's complete subservience *to* necessitating determination is surely *less* intelligible than are even the most sharply paradoxical theological accounts of the puzzles of human freedom and divine grace![22]

This paradox, let us suggest, is inherent in the function of science in our culture. For science appears in culture in two quite different roles: first, as a body of conclusions, theories, or hypotheses about the nature and interrelations of things, including man; and secondly, as a magnificent act of human creative rational autonomy, and, resulting from that creative activity of intelligence, as a means through which scientific man exercises a newfound control over his world, including his own species. Let us look at each of these roles in turn: We shall see that the first—the *knowledge* science produces—moves our thought about man inexorably in the direction of a total determinism, while the latter—the creative enterprise or *activity* of science—moves our thought about man inevitably toward emphasizing human freedom.

In the first role we are thinking of science as a body of conclusions or theories about the nature, functioning, and interrelations of the various objects of its inquiries. Here, in relation to inquiry about man, we are asking: What does science say about man? What do we know through science of our own nature, our origins, our capacities? Let us note that scientific answers to *these* questions always present to us a picture of a determined creature whose rise, organizational structure, functions, and powers are exhaustively explained within the terms of the causal nexus. Furthermore, the object is understood with regard to the observable and measurable forces that impinge upon it and work within it; it is spoken about only insofar as it is determined. The *subject* character of man when so studied, as self-caused or self-determining, thus tends to disappear under scientific scrutiny, or reappears only in the statistical tables of the social sciences, where it is at best only implicit or totally random. Thus as an object of scientific inquiry man is from the outset, by the nature of the method of scientific cognition, understood as a determined being.[23]

This is a valid aspect of man, and vastly informative. But let us note, when this view of man as a determined object is taken as an exhaustive explanation or description of man, it makes absurd and unreal the very language its perpetuators employ about the *uses* of this same knowledge. A scientific account of man as a purely natural product must perforce be regarded as abstractive and partial if we are to understand at all how the same man, the being we are talking about, proposes to use that knowledge intentionally and so for his own benefit.[24]

When, however, the scientific community considers not what it *knows* about man, but the creative *use* that knowledge might have for human purposes—when it is not science as knowledge but science as transformative activity that is considered—the gaze of the scientist is no longer on another man as the object of scientific inquiry. Now that gaze is on himself and the scientific community as a whole, on man the knower of objects through active manipulation, and by means of that knowledge, the potential controller of other objects and even of himself. He has ceased to look at man as the specimen in the laboratory or the patient on the bed; the scientist is now gazing at man introspectively in terms of himself and his colleagues, the men in the white coats. In the one case, of course, man appears as a small, passive, determined object in the blind flux of events; in the other, he enlarges into a wise, powerful, active, hence free subject, an Indra manipulating and directing the Flux —or at least having the ear of politicians in Washington— through his knowledge according to his own purposes.

The knower of science, as the rational and purposive manipulator of his environment, also knows through *self*-awareness all those capacities of intentionality and freedom which the most extreme idealistic, religious, or existentialist philosophies in history have ever claimed for man. Thus in that aspect of science where man appears as determined, the author or speaker is writing about man as the *object* he studies; in the aspect of science where man appears as almost infinitely free, he is writing or speaking about his own community of scientists and therefore about man as he is inwardly self-aware of him, as a rational and purposive *subject* manipulating reality intentionally. And so since mythical language has always been the natural, in fact inescapable, form of discourse with which we thematize the mystery of our own freedom and its uses, a mystery known, if at all, by self-awareness, it is no surprise that scientists, when they speak on the basis of their own self-awareness of their freedom engendered by scientific gnosis, should inevitably use the strange, paradoxical, unempirical, and utopian language of myth. Possibly, however, in understanding this same paradox of determinism and freedom, the Judeo-Christian symbols of the *creatureliness* of man and yet of his status as *imago Dei* may make more sense than does this contradictory modern picture of man as helpless patient in the backless hospital shift and yet as mighty doctor in the sacral white coat![25]

Not only is this myth radically paradoxical, if not contradictory—a problem not unknown in previous theology. It is, as is the case with most false myths, also morally extremely dangerous. Here in the ethical and social importance of the understanding of man as a personal being, as a child of God made in the image of God, we encounter a second use for Christian myths in a scientific culture.

The hope of many scientists for the future largely depends, as we have seen, on their confidence that through knowledge they can manipulate man for human purposes, much as man has already controlled natural objects in his environment. The model which articulates this hope for creative control through knowledge is that of the very successful application of engineering, biological, and medical knowledge to nature and to natural objects. Such use of knowledge for control over physical nature has until the present raised few moral problems, and so the model taken from engineering and medicine has seemed to validate over and over this hope for a better world through scientific technology. However, such problems as the pollution of the water, the air, and even the land of nature, the potential use of space in war, the possibility of military devastation of crops and the land, euthanasia, the potential use of live patients for transplants, and a host of other horrors just around the corner, suggest that technological control even over physical nature is not at all necessarily creative. The new knowhow may raise fully as many—and possibly worse—problems than it solves. Be that as it may, the application of scientific knowledge to natural objects has resolved untold important problems of agriculture, sanitation, medicine, architecture, and transport, and until the present raised few baffling moral or religious issues in so doing. Thus a model of the general problem of control through knowing structured in these terms has seemed to modernity generally to imply that little more is needed for creative control of human destiny than for man to enlarge his scientific understanding in relevant areas where scientific knowledge has been inapplicable so far.[26]

Control over *men* on a social scale, and thus control over society and through it over history, however, is a very different matter than control over nature, and it raises entirely different sorts of problems. In fact, it could be very dangerous indeed if this simple model of the engineer controlling inanimate nature when he plans a dam or a bridge is maintained when we move into the social uses of science. The technologist must come to realize that the *men* he seeks to control are not like the inanimate objects of engineering, but rather are as much characterized by personal freedom and rationality as is he, the knower. For this reason, because they are personal beings, control over men raises ethical and political problems unknown in engineering or in the laboratory.

One of the most significant things the humanities, and among them theology, can do is to keep reminding the scientific elite that when the latter produce schemes for the control of society and of man—through genetics, chemistry, or psychology—it is *fellow citizens* and not *objects* with which these schemes propose to deal; and that because this is so, the control of man's destiny through scientific knowledge is fraught with the political dangers of tyranny and the social dangers of the dehumanization of man. A strictly "scientific" view of man and his destiny, taken seriously, might tend to regard society as a vast laboratory, in which only the scientific manipulator and his political bosses retain their freedom.[27] The sciences of man can bring great benefit to the human venture, but only if in so doing the scientists are willing to grant to man as the *object* of their knowledge and control the same freedom and personal identity they presuppose themselves to have as the purposive knowers who effect that control.

Many psychoanalysts have provided us with excellent illustrations of this problem: Can the knower in the therapeutic session, the analyst, *control* the patient as the medical doctor might control the patient's body through organizing and directing its natural forces? Can he, even presuming he has the best intentions, "treat" his patient as a passive, natural object by manipulation? Or, as most of them have insisted, is this model, taken from engineering and medicine, totally inapplicable and even dangerous to the relation inherent in psychotherapy? Is not what the analyst can do merely that he can use his knowledge and skill to lead the patient to realize his *own* freedom, to become more deeply self-aware, and so to learn to control and direct *himself*?

Notice how here the model of the relation of knowledge and creative action is completely changed, and how the word "control" through knowledge has almost completely disappeared. Now our model is Socrates, the midwife, eliciting the free self-activity of the person analyzed. And the assumption is that one man can never work *directly* on the personal inwardness of another man without destroying him, without reducing him to the level of an object to be manipulated at someone else's will. He can only lead another man to self-realization, to the appropriation and use rather than the loss of his own freedom and self-activity.

If this be so, then the whole effort to understand the creative use of science on mankind in terms of objective knowledge leading to external control is a significant error; and more to the point, it is an error in our mythology and not in our knowledge or in our science. It is more in the mythology surrounding our capacities to *use* our knowledge creatively that our troubles with science arise than it is in our faith in man's powers to know. Science as cognition is relatively unalloyed in our history; science as power is potentially as ambiguous as is any other form of human power.

When we are dealing with social matters, with men and their destiny, all forms of objective knowledge must suffer transformation—they cannot be applied externally in terms of control over others as they are in relation to nature. Rather, they must be transformed so that they can be reappropriated by *each* human subject for and in his own freedom. The basic question, therefore, is not, as it is usually phrased by worried technologists: How can we, the educated rulers, use these new powers science gives us creatively and morally to control man's destiny? It is the much more baffling question: How can the truth we now know about man and his society be appropriated by mankind— by the citizenry of a state and by its lay political and social leaders—so that *they* can act in its terms freely and autonomously?

Thus has the problem of the use of science been translated out of the area of technology and external control into the deeper and more puzzling areas of education, of moral training, of politics, and of religion. And whether we speak of the issues of the use of atomic power, of genetic or psychological theories, or of social reform, *here* is the nub of the problem of control through the uses of science. For without passing through the freedom of each man concerned, by means of the arts of education, of politics, and of morals, even the most "moral" use of scientific power is dubious.[28] Fortunately, most members of the scientific and technological community who talk about future control over man and his destiny are far too good political liberals to mean a word of what they say—for in politics the word "control" quickly spells tyranny. A sense of the mystery and inviolability of the person, both in his personal and political relations, is necessary if we are to understand at all what scientific knowledge means to society both for good and for ill. A scientific culture can become demonic if science is not used by men whose self-understanding and thus whose public action is guided by symbols that transcend the limits of scientific inquiry and illumine the spiritual, personal, and free dimensions of man's being.

The third use of religious symbolism and so of theological reflection in a scientific culture concerns not so much the question of the preservation of the personal dignity of the object of control as it does the problem of the freedom and the wisdom of the controller himself. Theology can well point out that there is a good deal *less* freedom in the scientific knower and controller through his knowledge than most descriptions of the potential uses of science in the future seem to assume. It is strange but true that in this context theology stresses the determination of man, while the mythology of scientific modernity emphasizes his absolute and unconditioned freedom. Our suggestion, in other words, is that some of that sense of the determination of man's reason and will by forces outside and within himself, which determination is taken for granted in scientific accounts of man as an object, should be read back into their thoughts about scientific man as a subject, as knower and doer—when modern scientific culture speaks so glibly of controlling our destiny, of bending even evolution to our human purposes!

Knowledge is power. It results almost invariably in the power to control in some measure that which is now known. New knowledge about man can, therefore, lead to an increase in the power to control other men, and it is through that new potentiality for control that our knowledge appears to be able to direct human destiny itself. But new power, even power through knowledge, by no means guarantees the virtue or the wisdom of the controller, the self-control of the man who can wield the power. When men, even scientific men, exert social power over other men, they have left far behind the innocence of the laboratory, the engineering camp, and the hospital; now they have entered the murky and ambiguous realm of politics. And with regard to the uses of power in society and so in political life, the only valid experimental evidence about how men use power is given us by the study of history—not by the benign experiences of the scientist in his own laboratory.

History is, unfortunately, grimly unequivocal on one point, namely that power universally corrupts the users of power. The men who control others in the political arena are not so free to control themselves through reason and moral will as are those in the laboratory, or as they themselves assume. With regard to political and social matters, men are in fact determined by forces of ambition, of self-interest, and of anxiety about their class, nation, or race—

forces which twist the rationality of their minds and the morality of their wills, and which seriously diminish their control over what they do. The machinations of the physicians' union with regard to public uses of medical knowledge illustrates this change from the integrity of the office and the laboratory, to the unreasoned, prejudiced, and fanatic atmosphere of the political arena.

Somehow in history rational plans and good intentions seldom achieve full realization. Unlike corresponding plans in the laboratory, or at the space center, they become ethically muddied in their enactment, and create unintended evils as often as intended goods. Almost inevitably, whether we be idealistic revolutionaries against injustice or moral defenders of "freedom" and the status quo, in history we move from the innocence of moral intention to the corruption of actualization. Consider, for example, the vast difference in the success of its outcome between the War on the Moon and the War on Poverty; or consider how a host of noble revolutionaries such as Sukarno, Mao, Nkrumah, Castro, to name only contemporary examples, have become, some more and some less, corrupted tyrants in a few years' time; and saddest of all, how our own involvement with possibly the best of moral intentions in Vietnam has ended in an evil morass of death, fear, guilt, and cruelty.

Each illustrates the loss of control over what we are doing and over its moral consequences, a loss which seems endlessly to repeat itself.

In history men appear to have little control over what they do, for they cannot fully determine the ultimate direction and integrity of their own wills, much less the course of the history in which they are immersed. We can through technology wreck the entire country of Vietnam; but we cannot, whatever we will, achieve our goals there, nor can we even, were the will to do so there, extract ourselves from that guilty and suicidal morass. We controlled by decision our entrance into that portion of history; but all our technological and political experts cannot seem to direct an exit! The great increase in man's ability to control what is outside of him through technology has not led to any corresponding increase either in man's control over himself or over his historical fate. Rather, it is still true that in the political arena, an increment of power—of "freedom" in that sense—ironically tends to increase a man's bondage to his own self-concern, and thus to add to the fated destiny of what was unintended that he will bequeath to his children.[29]

One of the most vivid, ironical, and frightening examples of this sad truth about history—that even as mature technologists we have little control over our own intellects and wills, over our own acts, and so *ipso facto* over our resulting history—is the history itself of technology. Technology is perhaps the purest symbol of the victory of man's purposes over blind nature, of the victory of human intelligence and freedom over mere chance; it is thus the paradigm for the myth we are discussing. And yet look at technology. Ironically, it illustrates the deep ambiguity of all of man's powers and therefore of his history, combining possibilities for both good and evil, and even overlaying its own essence as an expression of human freedom with the implacability of determining fate. For technology itself has become one of the fates that haunt modern man, mocking his control over himself and even over nature. In fact, it has almost replaced blind nature as the main causative factor in whatever threatens our contemporary existence—it is worse, more hazardous to health and safety, to live in cities than in nature; and the rapid and uncontrolled development of technology is beginning to frighten many thoughtful technologists.

Technology is a powerful modern symbol of the ambiguity of our destiny, if not of fate, for three reasons. Each of these reasons represents the loss of the control by man's rational and purposive intentionality over the technology that man has created. Thus has human freedom, in creating technology, warped *itself* into a fate that has become a threat precisely to that freedom.

First, technology has the character of fate because the *fact* of the development or further expansion of technology cannot be stopped and is thus quite beyond human control. No political or moral force conceivable can prevent what is possible to be discovered and developed from being so; the further development of technology, whether we are pleased with its prospects or not, is as inevitable as any decree of the Greek Moira. New inventions, new developments in armaments, new improvements in industry, communications, and transport appear in a thousand laboratories and for a thousand reasons, economic and political. Thus as a whole their appearance on the scene of history is in fact unintended and unplanned; ironically, it is more an example of the irrationality of past history than of the "planning" that was supposed to be characteristic of the technological future. As a consequence, when one looks at the rise and progress of technology itself, it is very hard to see how the word "decision," so often used by writers on the subject of the uses of science, applies even remotely here.[30] Appearing thus quite without central or intentional control, the steady "progress" of technology obviously cannot be intentionally stopped; it is a fate about which "man" can do very little indeed.

Secondly, technology represents a modern form of fate because the *shape* or *direction* of this unstoppable expansion is also not under any measure of rational determination or control. The expansion of technology is literally a "frolic" of unplanned, erratic, arbitrary, and often trivial expansion.[31] New products, processes, and instruments are hourly developed which may at best waste our resources and labor, at worst work untold harm on the environment, on the economy, or on man. And yet no rational planning or moral calculation of the direction of this expansion is even contemplated. The course of technology represents, therefore, the height of contemporary *un*freedom, the point in our social existence where we probably have *least* intentional control over the shape of our destiny—for that destiny will in large part be determined by precisely this frolic of expansion. In political and economic life, not to mention the family future, ways have been worked out to reduce the utterly arbitrary character of our common march into the future. Technology seems the least subject to such intentional control, and thus what it brings to us in the days to come seems more of a "fate" than is almost anything else in our experience.

Finally, technology is a radical symbol for fate because the development and use of technology reveals itself to be the servant, not at all of our rational and moral wisdom, but rather of our bondage, that is, of our more sinful or greedy impulses—of the profit motive, of national pride, and of national or class paranoia.[32] In history the image of man as creative "technological man," wise and learned, manipulator of his environment, himself, and his destiny, gets muddied—as the stinging eyes and shortened breath of each modern technologist, coughing and gasping as he drives home from work through the smog, sadly illustrate.

Here lies perhaps the most important wisdom that theology might bring to a scientific culture. Just as man as a child of God is more *free* than scientific knowledge declares him to be, so even scientific and technological man, as a sinner among sinners, is more *determined*—by the social forces of class, nation, and race, and by the inward forces of greed, ambition, hostility, and anxiety for himself and his group— than those who unqualifiedly acclaim the benign social uses of our knowledge, and so who look contentedly and even complacently into our future, seem to assume. Only if a scientific society recognizes through some form of symbolization these two aspects of the mystery of man, only if it realizes the ambiguity with which its new knowledge and potent techniques can and will be used, can it with creativity deal with the ecological, social, political, and ethical problems which these new powers are now raising.

For if man has still great difficulty in controlling himself, even when he means well, then surely we must be much more realistic about ourselves and hence more careful when we embark socially on programs designed to control ourselves and thus our destiny and ourselves through scientific knowledge. The myth, in other words, of man come of age through an increase in his knowledge is not merely an inaccurate myth theologically. Even more, it is a dangerous myth in applied science. For if man believes this, and heaven help us if he does, then he will charge ahead to control and remake himself and his whole world, justifying himself all the while by his own good intentions, and yet actually, because he knows not what he does, controlling others for his own ends. On the basis of the validity of its realistic view of man, therefore, Christian theology can utter a most helpful warning with regard to the continuing need for social and moral control over the controllers.

A scientific age, which has added immensely to our understanding and to our powers, has not made us more virtuous, nor has it made the meanings of our life any more secure. Our control over ourselves and our consequent control over our own destiny seem in no wise to be more within our grasp than before. The old theological problems of the use man makes of his freedom, of his bondage to self-interest, and of the ultimate meaning of the human story have been dissolved neither by the physical nor by the life sciences. Rather they have been precisely increased by them.

As is well known, Greek philosophy, like modern mythology, tended to identify knowing with virtue or arete, our ability to know with our ability to solve significant problems and dilemmas. Though this Hellenic identification is also questionable (for example, see St. Paul's remarks in Romans 7), nevertheless it should be noted that Greek thought presents a better case than does the modern version of this gnostic hope.

Knowing, for Greek philosophy, was not *techne*, knowing how to do something; it was rather *wisdom*, knowledge of the self, of its structure or nature and its limits, and so knowledge of the eternal structures in which that nature of the self, in order to be fully itself, participates, becomes healed, and thus is enabled to become truly realized. Saving gnosis consisted not merely of our knowledge of objective interrelationships among things separated from the self, but precisely of knowledge of the order inherent in the self itself. Quite reasonably, therefore, it could be believed to lead to wisdom or self-direction, and so to virtue. Modern knowing in science, on the other hand, represents objective knowledge of external structures unrelated to the self, or to the mystery of its freedom. It thus totally overlooks the deeper problem of the self-control of the expert or the technologist. When, therefore, it promises a modern version of Plato's "ordered society,"[33] based on the wisdom of the scientific elite, it appears convincing only to those who have no deeper, or more credible, faith with which to view the future.

If man's actions, even or perhaps especially when he has gained great power through his knowledge, remain ambiguous in basic motivation and often tragic in their unintended consequences, then such action must be undertaken and understood in terms of a deeper framework if it is to be creative. As we noted, a consciousness of this ambiguity, even in our own actions, is necessary if we are not to go blindly on doing the evil we never intended to do; repentance in some sense is called for in every epoch—even when we are defending cherished values or even in the bright new world the young radicals are calling for. But then, when any generation, however secular, finally sees this ambiguity, and the inescapable selfishness that was its cause, they are apt to find their moral nerve cut. An angry helplessness about any creative action anywhere appears—and men withdraw from social history in despair, disgust, and shame, as another wing of the younger generation illustrates.

In every epoch of our history, then, we need to discover not only moral standards by which we may judge ourselves and the social world we live in, but also forgiveness somewhere for what we and our world are, an assurance of the ability to accept ourselves and our world, even in the ambiguity that we know to characterize them when we are aware of the truth. For only thus are we enabled to go on with our worldly work for a better and juster world than we now have. And in order to do *that*, we need to have a faith that something works for good, even beyond and within the mess that we men have made and will continue to make; we need an intelligible ground for hope, a credible "myth" that does not lie to us about ourselves and our future. Finally, if life is in this way made up of ambiguity and frequent conflict, we need to have an urge for reconciliation, with the others whom we have injured and with ourselves too. All of this points beyond the scope and capabilities of our own knowledge and of our own moral powers to the deeper sources of both, the God who is creative of our astounding capacities, who judges our waywardness, and who accepts our repentance; who works in the midst of our evil as well as of our good to further his purposes and fulfil his promises; and who calls us to reconciliation so that we may start again on his and our work for a better and a more humane future.

The vast new powers of science do not, in the end, make religious faith and commitment irrelevant; they make them more necessary than ever. And they make of the utmost importance the understanding and the use of the deeper symbols expressive of the real issues and so the realistic possibilities of man's destiny—the symbols of man's potentialities and nature as the image of God, of his waywardness as fallen from grace; of the judgment, the mercy, and the promise of God. For only on these terms can the mystery, the risk, and the hopes of the destiny of a scientific culture be comprehended and borne.

Man cannot believe himself to be the sole arbiter of his own destiny without intellectual contradiction and historical self-destruction. If he is to have confidence in his destiny, therefore, he must recapture that sense of the creativity, wonder, and sacrality of the given, as the source and ground of his own powers, of his potentialities, and of his hopes. And he must understand that the present and the future course of his history is not just the *servant* of his autonomy and creativity as in a "secular" understanding, but that in a mysterious way that destiny manifests as well He who is his Lord. For judgment on his misuse of his autonomous powers, and grace to re-create them, must be meditated to him through the events of his historical destiny if man is to have any confidence at all. The more he understands truly the mystery and the waywardness of his own freedom—the more he knows the truth of the symbol of his sin—the more ambiguous will the destiny science presents him become to him. For all an increment of knowledge can do is to increase the scope and the power of his freedom, and thus to increase the ambiguity that opens out in his future uses of these powers. Science does not answer the ultimate question of hope; it raises it more poignantly than ever.

An examination, therefore, of the uses of science reveals that inescapably, if we are to understand our future in the light of our growing scientific knowledge, we must move our reflection and thus our language to "deeper" issues: to the relations of an increased human power and freedom— however vast that increment—to sin, to judgment, and to the promise of renewal and fulfillment. And so finally we must begin to think of the entire eschatological scope of the work of divine grace in history. The dilemmas of even the most secular of cultures are ultimately intelligible only in the light of faith; the destiny of even a scientific world can be adequately thematized only in terms of religious symbols; and the confidence for the future even of technological man can be creatively grounded only if the coming work of the Lord in the affairs of men is known and affirmed.

To sum up our theme, every image of man points beyond itself to an ultimate horizon of being within which that image takes its place. It is theological as well as anthropological, it entails a cosmic and historical myth as well as a view of man. If nature, as secular culture sees it, is truly blind and pointless, then man himself takes on this sacral ultimacy and absoluteness, and sees himself as free and wise, as the Promethean godlet who can control history for his own ends and thus creates meaning and value *ex nihilo* out of the blindness of process. Such a pessimistic view of being and optimistic view of man is, we have argued, self-contradictory and unempirical, and thus doomed to collapse at the slightest breath of reality. If, therefore, we take a more realistic view of man as both free and determined, as both virtuous and ambiguous, good and sinful—as he is—then inevitably the grounds for historical hope, on which we all depend, must shift their balance, and, as in most human schemes of meaning, a cosmic, ontological ground of hope is discerned to balance the more realistic view of man.

This by no means proves there is a God, or an ultimate order or scheme to history and to social process. These cannot be proved. They can be discerned only by deep, involved intuition, by an apprehension of the wonder and meaning of the given structure of things in which our own reality and our own waywardness fit and find their place, and in which we find our creative task for the future. But that discernment or faith can arise, I believe, when we begin where we have begun: with a critical look at our images of man. And in that discernment of a wider sacral context of our human story, we can find grounds beyond our own intelligence and virtue for a hopeful answer to the question of our destiny. The immediate foreground of our destiny is, to be sure, dominated by our waxing powers of knowledge and control. Nevertheless, the ultimate horizon of our future is as shrouded in mystery as that of any other age, for the ambiguity of our freedom and our fate, and the strange way they can interact in history, remain as impenetrable as ever, giving to our feelings for the future the deep tone of anxiety. In our age as in any other, therefore, confidence and hope depend on a sense of the transcendent Lord of all things—for unless the Lord builds the house, the builders do labor in vain.

IV. Epilogue: Myth,
Philosophy, and Theology

In THE PRECEDING CHAPTERS we have approached the subject of myth indirectly. Recognizing that ours is a scientific culture for which mythical language is a problem if not an anachronism, we have sought to begin with the experience of a culture dominated by science, and from that perspective to see what the shape and role of myth might be for us today. In the process, we discovered that while science has transformed much of the essential character of modern mythical language, still it has by no means dissolved its own need for this kind of discourse. For in the understanding of science itself, both as a creative rational inquiry and then as the applied knowledge of man and his world, myth appears almost unwanted and certainly unexpected as the only means by which such understanding can be achieved.

If our more detailed argument on the basis of science and its role in culture has been valid, we have established that some mode of mythical or religious language is unavoidable and creative in the most secular of epochs. Our task now is to pull these strands together into a more explicit and consistent understanding of this mode of discourse in the contemporary setting. In order, however, thus to understand the contemporary destiny of religious language, we must bring another actor onto the stage. For philosophy has also had a transcendently significant role in the historical development of religious language, and this influence in all probability will not recede in the future. Let us begin, then, by attempting to assess the relative role of mythical and of philosophical language in the religious discourse which any culture finds inescapable.

As we maintained repeatedly, the mythical language of religion—in almost all its original forms—had two distinguishable characteristics. On the one hand, myth appeared linguistically as a *story*. The subject of the mythical narration, i.e., the actor or actors in the story, were spoken of as if they were beings within the continuums of space and time. Each god was linguistically a being, in fact a personal being: he had a past, often even parents, a definite character, purposes and intentions, alliances, problems, and hopes; (he or she) experienced the passage of past into present and into future (he remembered, he planned, he spoke, he promised, he acted, and then dealt with the consequences of his own actions and those of others). He dwelt in space, albeit a select and so transcendent space; he came to a place, hurried to another place; returned to his own abode, etc. We know who he was through what he did, and thus theology was narration, the telling of a story about his deeds that revealed the two important religious aspects of his being: his will or intention, and his power. On the basis of the story, our own obligations, possibilities, and hopes would be structured. In myth, then, religion portrays the divine as a being, as within the phenomenal matrix of space and time, and so as historical in character, acting dramatically in the world of nature and of other beings to further his own purposes.[1]

On the other hand, while its language points to things and persons within the phenomenal world, there is no myth whose *content* does not transcend that world. For myth speaks of beings and of deeds that founded not only the cultural world of ordinary experience, but the spatiotemporal continuum itself. Even when the myth deals with a "culture hero" and not an explicitly divine being, it moves our thought back to the beginnings, to those events when the present structures of our world were shaped, if not originated. Myth portrays the horizon or the ground of the life-world of man by telling the story of the origins of that world, and thus inescapably it points to what transcends the ordinary causal sequences of nature and of society to powers and events that brought them into being. Even the culture hero is not an *ordinary* fisherman, hunter, or warrior. As the original archetypal founder of that cultural form, it was he who brought this phenomenal order into being out of a preceding chaos, and thus in his own way he participates in the transcendence, the sacrality, and the ultimacy of an Indra or a Zeus. Thus mythical language is paradoxical: its language forms are phenomenal, historical, personal; yet its content points this usage beyond its ordinary usage to another realm.

Myth is the first step in the process of understanding man's deepest religious apprehensions; it is the prototype of theology.[2] Almost certainly myth is neither the first nor the most significant factor in religious awareness; for the desire to understand, while a peculiar and unique characteristic of man, is not the most fundamental level of his being. In all probability, religion originates objectively in deep prereflective levels of awareness, "prehensions" of the sacral forces on which man depends, combined with man's own deepest subjective responses to his world, responses both of joy, gratitude, celebration, and confidence or hope on the one hand, and of anxiety, terror, despair, and guilt or remorse on the other. Out of these communal "prehensions" and experiences of sacral powers and threats relevant to the ongoing life of man in the world—perhaps the forces of fertility, of rain, of animal life, of war, and all the host of cultural structures necessary to life—cultic actions and customs, prayers and incantations, and sacred norms for life certainly originally arise. At this level, divine fertility and "natural" forces, cult and cultural activity, religion and ethics, are scarcely differentiated. Man deals with his environing world, with his social organization, and with his own desires in terms of these religious actions called forth by his prethematic awareness both of the massive powers that encircle his life and also of the sacred gifts that enable him to order that life in relation to those powers and thus to continue it.

Myth organizes this total existence, this "world" which surrounds man, intellectually by setting it into its first reflective form. Through a story, it tells us how this structuring of sacred powers occurred, how space-time, nature and historical forces, receive this customary shape. Some myths explain the origin of the natural environment and its forces; some tell us of the founding of significant cultural forms. Since nature and culture are barely differentiated in man's mind, myth deals happily with either realm. Thus is myth, as we remarked, the prototype of theology.

Because of the radically undifferentiated form of early life, it is also the prototype of early cosmology (that is, of science as explanatory of our material environment, if not science as classificatory and pragmatic), of early philosophy as speculative about what is most original and therefore most real, of early history as knowledge of what has happened in our past to make us what we are. The history of the mythical language of religion since these early times has, we may say, reflected the slow separation off of these diverse cultural elements, each of which has subsequently become a separate "secular" discipline, leaving myth and theology in what seems to be a state of empty abstraction, in touch at best only with the ultimate or, if one be a contemporary skeptic, with nothing any more at all! Concretely in our first chapter we showed how the development of science, and correspondingly of historical inquiry, as specialized, semiautonomous disciplines with their own canons of inquiry, has removed the "factual" elements (cosmological and historical) from mythical language, leaving it uncertain of its referents and unsure of its validity and meaning.

The encroachments of scientific inquiry into the field originally held by mythical histories do not, however, represent either the earliest or the most paralyzing attacks against myth. For in any culture that has reached the level of explicit reflection, philosophy tends to challenge and then to replace myth as the appropriate way to understand and speak of the real, the transcendent, or the ultimate lying behind phenomena. No longer now are the structures of ordinary experience seen to come from the originating gods; now they are understood to arise from some deeper level of reality or process which is explanatory of their existence and order. We shall not try to describe the historical process in Hellenic culture in which this usurpation occurred, since this has been done by many other more learned and originative minds than ours.[3] Rather, recognizing the tendency of philosophy to transform and even to replace myth, let us raise two questions more relevant to our present theme, namely (1) what has been the role of philosophy in the explication of fundamental religious apprehensions, and (2) granting that role in the religion of any advanced culture, what might be left over for mythical language to do? If, as we have sought to show, theology is necessary for the creativity of a scientific culture, can theology in such a culture take any other than a purely philosophical form, and if not, why not?

As the early history of Christian reflection amply illustrates, the role of philosophy therein was at best ambiguous —necessary and thus creative in part, but also potentially warping in its ultimate effects. The union of the language of religion, in this case the traditions of late Hebrew religion, with Greek philosophy, was not merely accidental, as if it were the "bad luck" of the gospel that sooner or later it converted educated and so philosophical men. Nor was it merely that the Hellenistic culture into which Christianity emerged was philosophical in character, and thus that a religion that was adopted by that culture became in turn a philosophical religion.[4] On the contrary, the relation is essential and thus unavoidable. It derives from the character of religious discourse and of mythical language themselves, and becomes necessary to that language whenever the culture which bears and uses it reaches the level of systematic reflection, that is, raises in explicit form the problems of the meaning and the validity of its most fundamental language, its myths.

Perhaps the most essential meaning involved in the concept of the *development* of culture is the gradual appearance of self-consciousness, of rational reflection on the given forms of life within which men in a given culture live. Man is the being who questions, for whom his own being, its structures and those of his social and natural world, provoke him to thought.[5] He has, as we have already emphasized, a deep eros to know; and one of his most fundamental apprehensions of the sacred is as an order in his world which can be known and whose knowledge fulfills and perfects him. Thus as his self-consciousness develops and comes to flower, all that he participates in becomes an object of his reflection. He not only acts in order to exist, and feels his existence, and celebrates its sources in ritual and story; now he also sets that preunderstanding before himself as a problem. He seeks explicitly and so reflectively to understand his being, to thematize in systematic form his understanding of himself and his world, and to inquire about the validity of that understanding. The earliest forms of thought are reflective rationalizations of mythical pre-understanding, and out of this matrix philosophy and theology arise.

The process of exploring the meaning and the validity of mythical language, of the symbol system of a given religious tradition, is the task of theology. Theology arises inevitably within a religious tradition, therefore, whenever that tradition achieves the kind of self-development which can form a reflective culture around itself. And insofar as this task is undertaken at all, it involves inescapably a union with philosophical speculation, whose traditional subject matter concerns questions of meaning and of validity. The theological questions, What do our myths *mean* when they speak about the origins of things and the divine rulers of our destiny? and How is their truth related to the other truths we know? inevitably overlap with philosophical explorations into what is real in the passage of things, what is true in the welter of common deceptions, and what is good amidst all of life's desires. The moment man reflects on his religious beliefs, he is forced to achieve some measure of unity between these beliefs and the other realities with which he has to deal in experience and about which also he must reflect (in science and ultimately in philosophy) if he is to be man. The only other alternative is to live spiritually in two different worlds; but that is as destructive of his humanity as is the refusal to think. As man's physical, emotional, and moral existence each demand unity else he hardly be at all, so his reflective existence as well must achieve unity; and that drive toward unity of self-understanding, toward shaping into one horizon of conceptuality both himself and his whole world, impels myth into theology, and theology in turn into the arms of philosophy.

There is, furthermore, another more specific reason that human reflection on the meaning and validity of myth necessarily involves philosophical elements. As we have argued, mythical language has two aspects, paradoxically related to each other. On the one hand, its form is that appropriate to the explication of events in the phenomenal world, where personal or historical beings encounter one another in actions in space and time; on the other, its content points beyond "beings" to the originating and thus ultimate and sacral structures of being or reality. Myth is, from this point of view, a preontological or "ontic" ontology, that is, one set in the terms of the phenomenal world of ordinary experience.

If this be so, then the moment philosophical reflection appears on the scene, the status of myth, if the latter refuses union with, and transformation by, philosophy, is instantly reduced. Philosophical reflection searches out and uncovers the universal and permanent structures latent within the things and events of the space-time phenomenal world. Earliest reflection called these fundamental ontological structures the "origin" of things, showing its own recent appearance out of the mythical consciousness; but what was found was not just a divine actor or sacred event in the past. Rather it was an eternal, changeless, structural principle, or combination of them, continuously productive of the manifold of experience: Love and Strife; flux and Logos; infinite and finite; Ideas; Demiurgos and space; atoms and motion; forms and matter, etc., to name a few of the earlier alternatives.[6] As the universal structures of being, of what

is—the structures that must be present for a thing to be, as
Aristotle said[7]—these metaphysical or ontological categories
transcend in scope and in permanence the beings which inhabit space and time.

Naturally, therefore, whenever men have entered upon the
path of reflection, they find that the ultimate, the transcendent, and the sacred have for them shifted their ground
away from the divine beings of mythical language to these
universal structures uncovered by thought. The fact of this
shift is undoubted, evident in the outraged "prophetic"
criticism by these early philosophers of the myths as deroga-
tory to the divine.[8] Its underlying cause is equally apparent: the language of myth speaks of beings who do deeds
and who make events, and so who are apparently phenomenal in stature. Metaphysics, on the other hand, tells us
of the universal principles of all beings, and thus it speaks
of structures transcendent in universality and permanence
to these gods themselves. For the gods, now merely illustrating principles above them, have ceased to be the un-
challenged rulers of all that is. They have lost their ultimacy, their transcendence, and their sacrality; consequently,
as in the tales of the Greek gods and goddesses, these once
numinous realities have become lovely, lively, but profane
objects. The phenomenal and historical language of myth
has remained, but its content as pointing to ultimacy and
sacrality has dissolved away, this aspect of its role having
been usurped by philosophy. Henceforth, if one is to speak
at all of the transcendent and the divine, it must be at least
in terms of these universal structures of things which now
mediate that which is ultimate and sacred to an age when
reflection has appeared.

Thus, far from threatening the religious profundity of
the young Christian faith, the introduction of philosophical
categories into the religious discourse of the early Christian

community was necessary if the transcendence and sacrality of God were to be there expressed. Insofar, on the one hand, as the Christian religion worshiped a god who was believed to be creator of, and sovereign over, the beings of the world, and insofar, on the other, as the claim of the gospel was that it offered redemption to man and to history as such, and not just to a particular group of men in a particular history, that is, insofar as the Christian God was really ultimate and his power and sovereignty truly universal, it was necessary that Christian modes of reflective speech express a maximum of transcendence, universality, and permanence.

Beginning with almost the earliest of the Greek Fathers (Philo the Jew was the first!), and stemming through Augustine's influence in the Latin world, Christian language about God employed the philosophical concepts of Stoicism, middle Platonism, Neo-Platonism, and then Aristotelianism[9] in order to express the transcendence of God as the source and ruler of all things, and the activity of God in the world. Yahweh thus became "God," a transcendent yet personal reality who is necessary being, *a se*, pure form, changeless eternity, nameless, etc.[10] Correspondingly, in its discourse about man, history, and the Incarnation, theology used the philosophical categories again of Stoicism, Platonism, and Aristotelianism to express the essentiality and universality of the Christian claim that in God's action in Christ all men and all creatures are redeemed for all eternity. Thus the Wisdom of God became the divine Logos; Adam was elevated to the status of the Idea of man, the symbol and source of human nature itself; and Jesus revered as at once not only the new embodiment of that Idea, but also the incarnation of the transcendent Logos of God.[11] In each case philosophical categories were added to historical and mythical ones to express divine ultimacy, decisiveness, universality, and permanence.

On the other hand, the particularity of the Christian religion, and its basis in definite historical events, forced this now largely philosophical theological language to retain certain "mythical" elements in each of its fundamental statements of its *regula fidei*. In its affirmation of creation *ex nihilo* and at a first moment of time (both very *un*philosophical notions) ; in its emphasis on a *historical* Fall; and above all in the recitation of the subsequent wonders of *Heilsgeschichte*—those past events of revelation, incarnation, and resurrection, and those future promises of an eschatological end—a *story* (or "economy") of salvation was told. In this story eternity and time, the transcendent God and particular moments, were bewilderingly combined. Thus even in the most philosophical of the Fathers, "mythical" elements expressive of this *temporal* activity of God, and matter-of-fact elements expressive of the *particularity* of the events recited, remain.[12] But intertwined with these remaining elements of personalistic, historical, factual, and so mythical forms of language were inescapable and hence creative philosophical elements that pointed to the transcending traits of ultimacy and sacrality also intrinsic to these religious and theological meanings.

This is not to deny that the inordinately supranaturalistic and spiritualistic tendencies of Greek philosophy threatened the personalistic, historical, and materialistic traits of Biblical religion. Nevertheless, had these philosophical elements not been there at all, Christianity would have been quite unable to speak validly of its God who, as well as "acting" in history, at the same time transcended history, nature, and the beings who peopled the world of ordinary experience. In truth, Christianity would have been a "cult" whose deity was only one beneficent being in the universe, quite lacking in ultimacy and universality, and such a cult would have been quite incapable of surviving the collapse of a culture formed on other ultimate grounds. The same requirement that theology be "ontological" as well as "ontic," so that its language about God, the world, and man achieve the necessary universality and permanence to transcend the immediate structures of being, is present today as it was in the first five centuries—lest again God be a being less than ultimate, and lest his promises be a mere palliative in a world beyond his own final control.[13]

The relation of philosophy to the sacred dimension borne by mythical discourse is, however, a paradoxical one. In a sense, philosophical reflection transcended the mythical tradition and formed its own relatively abstract notions of deity, notions which were more universal, more permanent, and more ultimate than any which the ontic language of myth had been able to achieve. But in another sense, philosophy itself reaches its nemesis in seeking to express the transcendent and the sacred. For speculative philosophy searches for and uncovers the universal structures of being, those principles which are evident everywhere since they are essential if anything is to be at all. Such principles transcend, as we noted, the ontic realm of beings: flux or matter are more universal principles than Tiamat, and Ideas or Logos than Indra or Zeus. Nevertheless, these structures of being, universal and necessary though they be, are in the last analysis themselves immanent structures; they define the most permanent and universal characteristics of the given system of things, but they have difficulty expressing anything that transcends that system as its ground, source, or end.[14]

Greek philosophy itself realized this. Plato, having practically outlawed religious myth in the ideal society, brought back philosophical myth as the sole way to deal with the transcendent mysteries of existence. Aristotle's god was defined in as transcendent terms as philosophy allowed, but still it was clearly a part of the total system of things, and consequently before it was transformed by medieval speculation, the Unmoved Mover never achieved any religious role. Thus when in the Hellenistic age religious feeling returned in overwhelming power and yearned for some "object" of real transcendence and sacrality, such transcendence was found only through a principle that transcended philosophy itself, in the Neoplatonic One that lay beyond the realm of Logos and so beyond all the categories of reflective thought whatsoever. Thus the One in late Hellenistic thought is philosophically "nameless"; all that can be said of It is said, on the one hand, by negating philosophical discourse, and, on the other, by a kind of queer, transmuted mythical language.

In the *Enneads* of Plotinus the One is in the first instance declared to be beyond being and nonbeing, beyond all form, beyond the subject-object distinction, and so beyond all thought, and beyond the soul and its motion—and thus is it philosophically nameless.[15] On the other hand, to express the relation of the One to the world it transcends, a relation necessary if the *one* is to be philosophically explanatory of the world and its structures, the One is said to "overflow," to "be without envy," and to be "the Good," the object of all striving and eros.[16] In the latter phrases mythical or ontic language has clearly reappeared at the extreme height of Hellenistic philosophical speculation about the transcendent. To be sure, such speculative thought, in declaring that the relation of the One to space and time is one of "overflowing," has no intention of making reference to special divine deeds, to special times and places, and so to any "factual" language. The relation which is the referent of this speech is an utterly universal and timeless relation. Nevertheless, this is "phenomenal" (ontic) and so mythical speech, that is, it is a description of that which founds all facts and principles in the terms of words ordinarily used to describe beings or events in space-time (e.g., overflowing, envy, plunging, rising, falling, etc.) Philosophical negation of philosophical terms is used to express the transcendence of the One, and then mythical categories are employed to reexpress now in this purified realm its eternal and changeless relatedness to the beings of experience. Thus, as this strange history shows, while religious discourse on the reflective level must use philosophical language to point *beyond* the beings of our world, beyond ourselves and our immediate environment, religious thought—in this case mystical religious thought—in transcending the universal images of speculative philosophy, returns to a new, rarefied usage of the mythical when it seeks positively to be expressive of genuine ultimacy and sacrality.

In theological discourse expressive of the religious faith of Judaism or of Christianity, this postreflective use of mythical categories has an even firmer basis in the essential character of these religions themselves. For the basic experience of God originative of these forms of piety is not a mystical experience of transcendence beyond the phenomena of the world; rather it lies in historical events themselves taken to be revelatory of the activity of the transcendent God within history itself.[17] Thus central to their expression of the nature of the divine are elements expressible only in ontic or mythical categories, in this case personal and historical language.

On the one hand, since special events are involved here (the Exodus, the Incarnation, the promised fulfillment at the end), there is postulated a freedom or a personal depth in God transcendent to all universal structures of existence whereby he can "enter" the system of the world at a given place and time while at the same time universally and at all times upholding that world.[18] On the other hand, for the same reason, since the activity of this "free" God in the concrete, phenomenal character of history (at *this* crossing of the Red Sea, in *this* man born of Mary, dead before Pilate, and risen again) must also be expressed theologically, again mythical language is necessitated to express the divine activity in these special events (for example, God called Moses, parted the waters, sent his son, and raised Jesus from the dead).[19] Thus in these traditions the divine is described not only philosophically in terms of its changeless and universal relations to the beings (as in Neoplatonism and other mystical religions), but even more centrally he is described "mythically" in terms of his special deeds in the midst of the historical and phenomenal realms themselves.

Clearly in the case of such religious traditions, mythical language about "divine deeds" and "crucial events" in space and time is not simply transcended as a primitive mode of religious language, to be replaced by pure reflective discourse, first by the categories of metaphysical speculation and then by the endless negations and the eternal metaphors characteristic of Neoplatonism and classical Hindu reflection. Rather, here mythical language returns as essential to all that is to be said about God.

In Christian theological discourse, therefore, there is an almost infinitely complex interrelation of mythical and philosophical elements.[20] Let us try to sort these out before we add scientific language to enrich our brew. Christian theology must contain philosophical or ontological elements: (1) in order that the ontological uniqueness, universality, and decisiveness of God to each creature be adequately expressed, that is, in order that *God* be properly conceived theologically; and (2) in order that the universality and the decisiveness of the problem to which religion addresses itself and of the resolution which is offered be expressed, that is, in order that its *salvation* be properly conceived theologically. Thus some form of general ontology, some philosophical view of man's nature, and some form of philosophy of history must be implicit in any Christian theology that is internally consistent and externally intelligible.

On the other hand, Christian theology must retain mythical elements for two reasons: (1) In order that the ultimacy, freedom, and transcendence of the divine over the system of things be expressed in determinate and not merely in negative terms. Any philosophical expression of the divine that is not merely negative is inescapably analogical or metaphorical in form, and such use of analogy, being "queer" from the point of view of speculative philosophy, implies and requires ultimately a mythical mode of language about God.[21] If thought is to transcend the system of beings, as it must if it expresses the sacred, it must paradoxically relinquish ontological speech and return to a rarefied, analogical ontic speech. For only the ontic, the phenomenal, and the historical can express the absolute uniqueness and the intentionality of the sacred on the one hand, and its strange and unique relatedness to the beings on the other—a uniqueness that is not merely that of one being among the many beings and a relatedness that is not merely the reciprocity of the beings one to another. Since ontological categories "taken straight" confine thought to the reciprocities among the plural entities of the given system, these categories, like undiluted ancient myth, culminate in a purely profane system of thought which fails to express the divinity of the divine. Thus even in the most sophisticated philosophical theology, myth returns to express the height of the divine transcendence and sacrality and its unique omnipresent and everlasting relatedness to the universal structures of what is.

(2) Christian theology must contain mythical categories because its understanding of the transcendence and the sacrality of the divine is grounded in particular past events

within the general stream of temporal passage and contains promises for the particularity of history in the future. God here is thus related to *particular* events, and at the most *concrete*, phenomenal level.[22] Insofar as these categories are both historical and decisive for Christian understanding, that unique role is expressible only when the immanent categories of historical inquiry and explanation, that is, when descriptions of ordinary, historical "facts," make some form of union with the suprahistorical categories of myth. Thus whenever Christian theology speaks of God's relation to particular historical events, it combines, on the one hand, the purely factual language of historical narration with, on the other, the mythical language of deeds and acts, of purposes and of promises[23]—lest all either be reduced to finite causality or else the sacred remain unrelated to the particularity of history. And further, since both judgment and redemption are received in the present, and in promise for the future, on the ontic or phenomenal plane of history characterized by actual temporal passage, again mythical speech is necessary when the relation of the divine to ourselves in the present and our hopes for the future are explicated. Philosophical conceptuality, because of the utter universality of its categories, tends to negate as relevant to truth universally not only the transcendence of the divine over the structures of natural things, but even more the concreteness, decisiveness, and uniqueness of particular events and histories in the passage of time.

Consequently, Christian theological language has both ontological and ontic elements, both metaphysical categories and mythical narrations. Almost every great theologian has combined these two elements in some balance; in some theologians the ontological predominates, and the ontic or mythic only appears at crucial points of transcendence or of divine activity—as in Augustine, Thomas,

Schleiermacher, and Tillich. In others, the individual and mythical have predominated and ontological categories then recede to the background, qualifying the ontic language about God and thus raising him to a status of transcendence and universality far above the beings of ordinary experience —as in Luther, Calvin, Ritschl, and Barth. Probably this argument will go on interminably, the drive for cosmic universality and significance seeking to replace the mythical elements with ontological categories, and the claims of ultimacy and of historical uniqueness continually reinstating the mythical as determinative of its philosophical components. Undoubtedly, Christian theology, based as it is on a particular religious awareness born of a past history but taken to be of universal significance for all men as to what is ultimately real, must contain both elements; it is thus vain and self-defeating to seek to make it either purely philosophical or purely mythical and ontic in its form.

In sum, Christian theology came into the modern world with three related ingredients characteristic of each of its major doctrines: (1) A mythical or ontic element expressive, on the one hand, of the ultimacy, transcendence, and sacrality of God: his creative power and sovereignty, his essential freedom over himself and his world, his eternal intentions and purposes, his transcending and creative love; and, on the other hand, expressive of the particularity and concreteness of the relations of God to particular historical events. (2) A philosophical element partially explicative of the transcending and ultimate aspects of his deity, varying in its form with the period and the school of philosophy represented. And (3) a "matter-of-fact" element derived from (a) the earlier, purely mythic form of Biblical speech, and (b) the relation of Christian discourse to special events and histories. For example, classical theology spoke of such essentially "ontological" doctrines as creation, fall, and salvation in terms of the six days of Creation, the factness of Adam's Fall, and the historicity of the Exodus, the Conquest, the Incarnation, and the Second Coming. In the modern period, this threefold form of language found itself challenged for really the first time by the growing significance of scientific discourse. The nature of this interaction formed the subject of our first chapter; let us here summarize that discussion.

Science, we found, has had a paradoxical relation to theological language. In the first place, it has removed from theology, and also from purely religious speech, all claims to inform us on its own authority of any matters of fact ingredient to religious assertions. Mythical language no longer claims to tell us of the existence or nature of any events, past or future, however significant they may be for the meaning and validity of their associated religious beliefs. It may, to be sure, tell us that given certain events— e.g., the "facts" of Jesus' life and death—their ultimate meaning and even the ultimate cause of them is of such-and-such a nature—namely that God sent his Son to redeem man. But no Biblical or dogmatic proposition as such can *inform* us on its own authority of any set of natural or historical matters of fact. Thus, as we saw, did science separate the mythical language of traditional theology about God's acts in nature and history from the immediate and observable system of finite interrelations in which we actually live, and correspondingly religion seemed to tell us nothing more about the world we live in than we knew before.

As we noted, however, the development of science effected more changes in religious language than merely removing the latter's capabilities of initiating factual statements. For gradually, as it rose to dominance in our cultural life, science created a new attitude to knowledge and thus to the fundamental conceptions of reality and truth characteristic of modern culture. As a mode of knowing, science increasingly depended on an empirical base and an empirical validation for all of its fundamental hypotheses: what could be known by science, and thus what for a scientific culture was "real" as the subject matter of valid propositions, more and more become continuous with immediate and shareable experience. For only in such experience could anything at all be uncovered by the methods of science and any statement tested.

Strangely, therefore, as the power of scientific inquiry to know the natural world expanded incredibly, a countermovement appeared to develop: the power of man's mind to know "reality" seemed to shrink. The history of modern philosophy, from the seventeenth century onward, illuminates this shrinkage. Steadily the confidence that man can speak intelligently about Being, "ultimate reality," substance, and the eternal or universal structures of existence diminished. Instead of being one aspect or one school of philosophy, critical empiricism became philosophy's major tendency and practically its definition. All propositions that are meaningful are those which originate in direct shareable experience and can be tested therein. Any other form of statement has moral, psychological, or emotive relevance only. Science informs us of objective reality; religion informs us at best of man's own ideals and dreams, at worst of his neuroses; and metaphysical speculation being neither as verifiable as are scientific hypotheses nor as emotively revealing as religion, is apparently of little interest to anyone. Philosophy culminates as the analysis of the logic and the language men use in their other concerns; but it possesses no power to *know* a wider, deeper, or more enduring structure than does empirical science.

The counterarguments of speculative philosophy concerning the necessity of metaphysical thought for our wider cultural life are, it seems to me, unanswerable. These arguments are that otherwise that culture's cognitive, ethical, aesthetic, psychological, and social experience is founded irrationally and uncritically on principles and perspectives of which the culture is unaware, and which are as irrational as were the myths from which science was purported to have freed mankind.[24] Ironically, with the development of positivism, language philosophy, and a radical existentialism, cultural life manifests, now on a more sophisticated level, its own most primitive because unself-conscious form. For now without speculative philosophy its own essential structures of life remain unreflected upon, and its own most fundamental principles unthematized.

It is a further irony of our scientific age that most creative members of this culture do not accept these arguments for a speculative philosophy. Science, social science, and even philosophy in our day ply their trade without feeling the need for any epistemological or ontological foundations whatsoever. Thus Auguste Comte turns out not to have been so naïve as was once thought when he prophesied that as metaphysics had replaced myth, so science would remove the need for metaphysics.[25] While his delineation of these three stages of thought in all probability was no veridical prophecy of the total direction of human culture as such, it appears to have been a fairly accurate assessment of the effects on Western thought of the development of science as the dominant, paradigmatic form of knowing.

Recent history has thus in part validated Comte's insight that metaphysical speculation is in fact a rationalized form of the mythical, religious consciousness, the form that that consciousness takes in a sophisticated and so reflective culture. For metaphysics has largely retained what vitality it preserves in our culture as the ally, if not the instrument, of religion. The essential contribution of ontology to the elaboration of a theological perspective has turned out to be the major role the metaphysician has enjoyed in the twentieth century. Although in theory metaphysics is equally foundational for any special discipline,[26] it enjoys no such recognition with regard to its corresponding function in science, art, ethics, or political and social thought. Only theologians seem to absorb and use the creative metaphysical systems of our time—for only the religious community seems to feel the need to maintain cognitive touch with those structures of ultimacy which found our being and which it is the classic role of metaphysics to describe.

Now the main significance of this development for our present theme is that a scientific culture appears to make difficult and irrelevant all statements about the universal, the necessary, the transcendent, and the sacred in existence. Such statements, being expressive of the bases of scientific inquiry, are not subject to the methods of scientific inquiry itself. Thus have both the traditional mythical symbols of our religious communities, and the traditional metaphysical structures of our philosophical history, dissolved together. "God" and metaphysics "died" in the West in approximately the same half century; and it is not at all strange that this death took place during the period in which science rose to universal cultural dominance as the paradigm of knowing and thus the arbiter of the real and the true.

The problems, not to say crises, which current theology faces, therefore, involve all *three* of its constituent elements and not just one or even two of them. Not only has theology been forced to adjust itself to a radical loss of authority with regard to its factual elements, an adjustment outlined in the first chapter. Even more it has had to reappraise its peculiar forms of meaning and of validity in an age in which *both* mythical and metaphysical assertions are widely suspect since they appear to be irrelevant at best and meaningless at worst, a theme partially explored in the third chapter. Theology's problem is not merely that it is too literalistic for a scientific age, so that a modernization will save it, as liberalism believed; nor is it that it is too metaphysical in an age that scorns metaphysics, so that founding it only on the mythical language of revelation will safeguard it, as neo-orthodoxy insisted; nor is it even that it is too "mythical" (revelational) for modern man so that translation into metaphysics will cure its ailments, as Hegelians, Thomists, and Whiteheadians have promised. It is that all three of its traditional constitutive elements seem to have lost their significance and their legitimacy in a theological context for a scientific culture.

It was for this reason that we attempted to analyze science itself with regard to both of the creative roles which it assumes in modern culture, roles which are central foci of our contemporary culture's life. These two roles are: (1) that of knowing what is the case in our world through the organized and shareable methods of scientific inquiry, and through the development and testing of theoretical hypotheses; and (2) that of resolving practical problems through the application of this knowledge to ecological, biological, psychological, and social problems. For much of modernity science in both of these roles has already demonstrated not only the untruth of ancient religious myth but even more the irrelevance of religious convictions. Since no divine beings could, even in future inquiry, be uncovered or described by scientific exploration, how, granting that science is the paradigm of modern knowing, can religious referents be anything but empty and meaningless in such an age? Nor apparently is there any limit to the kinds of problems that an advancing technology can resolve, so that religious help to resolve life's crises seems as vain as the hope that it can inform us of truths we do not otherwise know.

As we showed, however, an analysis of science, both in its cognitive and its technological roles, uncovers dimensions within scientific experience itself which the categories of science, its modes of understanding either itself, its world, or its possibilities, are ill-equipped to clarify. As the ground of its own possibility as a cognitive endeavor, a dimension of ultimacy appears inescapably in science, and in the end the only way this foundation for all acts of knowing can itself be understood is through categories similar to those we have called mythical. The traditional role of myth as explicative of the transcendent and the sacred as it manifests itself in and through the finite, is as necessary today as it was in prescientific cultures, lest the ground of science itself, the foundation of this paradigmatic act of human cognitive creativity, be itself unexplicated and uncelebrated.

Correspondingly, the use of science by technological man to resolve his own historical problems and thus as an aid to the mastering of his destiny, raises a host of issues which only the language of religious myth can clarify. When technology is given historical application, immediately the *mystery* of man's freedom in relation to the forces that determine him; the *paradox* of his character and status as a person who thinks and decides as well as an object of theoretical investigation and technical manipulation; the *tragedy* of his bondage to anxiety and self-concern and his strange inability to control himself; and thus the *ambiguity* of his destiny even when he freely seeks to control it—all of these evidences of the mystery of our existence appear. And each one of these evidences has this element of mystery and of uncontrollability within it because it points to a dimension of depth in our human being that scientific knowing and common experience cannot explicate. And as myth has always thematized man's experience of the transcendent and the sacred, so it has alone been the linguistic mode with which man can reflect upon his own freedom, his person-ness, his evil, and his destiny—an inevitability more than established by the appearance of scientific myths in the bosom of a secular culture. Thus a proper understanding of science calls for a deepening of the mythical conscious-ness if a scientific culture is to realize its potentiality; it does not call for its eradication.

It would take another volume to show that, granted the necessity in a scientific culture for both scientific inquiry and the mythical elaboration of the horizon within which this inquiry functions, philosophical analysis is itself required. Suffice it here to say that in our day, science and myth cannot function without the meditation of philosophy.[27] If myth expresses the dimension of ultimacy in experience, and the mystery of human knowing and doing, if its "object" is the transcendent and the relation of our freedom to the transcendent, then as we noted, ontological language is required in order that this mythical discourse ascend to the necessary level of generality and of universality where the transcendent genuinely appears. Unless this ascent is made, myth functions merely as pre-science, a phenomenal expla-nation for phenomenal experiences—and it will be speedily dissolved by the developments of new scientific inquiry.

Correspondingly, if it be so that both as inquiry and as technology science genuinely rests on a foundation which cannot be explicated scientifically but whose thematization is necessary for intelligence to function, then again phi-losophy is essential if scientific man is to understand and wisely to use his amazing powers to know.

Thus the three elements of traditional myth, metamor-phosized into three diverse forms of modern culture, require one another: the inquiry into matters of fact, the observable structures of the spatiotemporal continuum, being the domain of science; the inquiry into the fundamental hence universal structures of knowing itself, and so of the finite being which is known, being the task of transcendental analysis and of ontology; and finally the explication of the horizon of ultimacy, the mystery and tragedy of freedom and the sacred grounds of confidence and hope, being the task of religious myth and of theology.

We should sum up this essay on myth, science, philosophy, and theology with a final word about the current character of theology as a mode of language in such a cultural situation. This is of course a vast subject; in the light of our present discussion, one final point needs to be clarified. Granted that science has historically and irreversibly usurped the role of declaring and describing matters of fact, how does the "factual element" characteristic of all previous mythical and religious language arise and take its place in the modern religious consciousness, and so in contemporary theological reflection on that experience?

All language must relate to direct experience if it is to be meaningful and in some measure testable. Correspondingly, the events which myth relates must be in some continuity with the space and time in which we live if their religious symbols are to be explanatory of our actual existence. But in an age when scientific inquiry is granted jurisdiction over all events in the spatiotemporal continuum, how can myth be meaningful on these terms? How can it avoid floating above actuality like a fantasy, as idle dream or as tortured projection, its only touch with factuality its origin in our churning subconscious? In answer we may postulate that the factual element of myth takes three forms in contemporary life, corresponding to the fundamental phases of our temporality and of the essential structure of Christian belief. All of these points of contact with concreteness are essential both to meaningful religious speech and to cultural wholeness.

First of all, as our argument throughout has implied, religious myths are related to present factuality, to the manifold of immediate experience, at those places in ordinary experience where a dimension of ultimacy manifests itself either as creatively present or as devastatingly absent; where man experiences an ultimate grounding of his powers and so a basis for his creativity, his confidence, and his hope—or, alternatively, where he experiences an ultimate threat to his powers, and hence the spectators of ultimate doubt, despair, and meaninglessness. Generally in modern life, cut off by its secularity from explicit celebration of the sacred, these experiences arise only negatively, that is, when we encounter the *limits* of our powers, or when the *ambiguity* of what we are overwhelms us—when, that is, we know, as Tillich put it, "the shock of nonbeing." Speaking ontologically, these experiences appear as connected with our awareness of our contingency, relativity, and temporality, and our consciousness of the utter ambiguity of our freedom—or, to put this in mythological language, when man encounters his three most ancient enemies: fate, sin, and death. But where a sense of grace has been allowed to develop, such experiences can arise in positive form as well: again in connection with our ontological structures of contingency, relativity, temporality, and freedom—for example, in experiences of birth, of being alive, of meaning, of finding some aspect of truth, of obligation and responsibility, of forgiveness and self-acceptance, and of a new reconciliation with others and the world.[28]

These are "ordinary experiences" which are quite concrete, whose positive and negative powers shape the factual character of all secular existence, as fully in a scientific culture as in other cultures. Such experiences, and the ontological structures they reflect, are what religious discourse is "about"; they map out the area of ordinary experience to which religious symbols apply and which (in this sense) these symbols "mean." They thus provide the necessary concrete or factual elements to any system of religious language so that it can both be meaningful and communicate a sense of validity to those who believe in its symbols. One aspect of the task of theology, which is reflection on the symbolic, mythical discourse of a particular religious tradition with regard to its meaning and validity, is precisely to relate that system of symbols to these relevant regions of ordinary experience, and thus to clarify the meanings of the religious symbols which it seeks to explicate.

No set of religious symbols, however, is taken by its adherents to arise merely from ordinary or present experience, though their meaning or application may lie there. Significant religious symbols—and the myths that group them together into "stories"—arise in special experiences where an unusual encounter has taken place, where the transcendent and the sacred has manifested itself in a special manner—and thus can be redemptive of those ills of ordinary experience with which ordinary powers cannot cope. Such unusual experiences of the sacred ground of our being and our powers have been universal. Each of them, if it be a significant "hierophany" of the sacred, has been productive of a new understanding of existence, a new stance of life, and thus ultimately of a new community and a new cultural form. Religious symbols point to, and thus transmit or communicate, this manifestation in the past of the ground of things, and thus continue these religious and cultural forms in the communities that embody them in historical time.

Thus a special history of past events, symbolic forms, and

community together establish our cultural and religious life—and each community that represents a mode of being in the world, whether it be a political, scientific, artistic, or religious community, treasures its crucial past, its ruling myths, its normative standards, and seeks to pass them on to its children. Inescapably, then, a factual element accrues to any set of religious symbols because these arise out of a series of special past events borne into the present by a tradition. A Jewish or Christian religious community—like a liberal political community—is re-created through a reappropriation, a recelebration, and a reenactment of its own crucial past. The transcendent and the sacred, experience of which founds and sustains human and thus cultural existence in all its facets, is communicated to us through our communal histories, through the symbols and the forms of the community's life in which we spiritually exist. Inescapably, therefore, any living religious symbol in such traditions, has, as part of its meaning and crucial to its validity, reference to the factuality of the past, and especially to those events creative of that tradition.

Another task of theological reflection, therefore, is to sort out the problems arising for religious symbols from this interaction of past history with our present experiences of transcendence. In this interaction, the concreteness and specificity of our past, requiring the arts of historical inquiry, mix uneasily with the universality, objectivity, and scope required of each present appropriation of the ultimate that comes to us through that past. There are no easy solutions to the problems of historical inquiry and the present witness to divine revelation, of the radical particularity of the past and the claim of universality, and of the paradox of concrete phenomena through which transcendence manifests itself. And of course different communities, and different theologies, with their different symbolic forms, will emphasize these two polar elements differently. Some find the essence of their answer in the special, historical, particular, and "phenomenal" character of special events of the past—and thus encounter more trouble with history and science, and with the requirements of universal thought. Others find the essence of their answers in the present universality and scope of Christian symbols—and thus find it difficult, on the one hand, to treasure the significance of the historical and the particular, and, on the other, to appreciate either the ambiguity and tragedy of the ordinary or the wonder of its rescue by transcendence.

The difficulties in the relation of religious symbols to history are thus legion, but utterly, in our view, inescapable. Man is a historical being as well as a religious one. He appropriates ultimacy not only in the process of living through events in present time, but his stance vis-à-vis transcendence is always a historical stance, given him by a community with a tradition; and his humanity is such that every appropriation of ultimacy in past and present projects him into a future which his freedom will in part form. Thus, however universal his vision of the ultimate horizon of things, that vision, and the language with which he expresses it, and the elements of experience that make it valid for him, have all arisen historically, and consequently are rooted in the factuality and particularity not only of his biography but even more of his communal history. A contemporary theology, therefore, reflecting on the mythical structures that give meaning to present existence, will of necessity have to understand these symbolic meanings in relation not only to *present* secular experience but also in relation to the particularity and concreteness of special historical experiences in the *past*.

Finally, as we noted in the third chapter, Biblical and also religious myths, and so the theology that reflects on them, have a *future* as well as a past and present reference, and here again the reference is factual as well as transcendent. This future reference in Biblical religion has many roots: a new dynamic view of God in his activity, a new history-centered context for understanding the meaning of life, and a new orientation to time and process as reaching toward a promised goal. All of these—the new understanding of God, of man, and of temporal history, have given Biblical and modern religiosity a forward rather than a backward look.

Probably as decisive as any of these is the fact that the religious symbols of the Judaeo-Christian tradition relate themselves to man ethically as well as ontologically. That is, they communicate a demand, a judgment, and a call, and correspondingly they include not only a recital of past events, and an experience of present grace, but also a divine promise for the future. In relation to these symbols, therefore, human freedom is called forth in action toward the future, and correspondingly the divine grounds for that autonomous action are presented: the power and the faithfulness of God, and his promise that that power and intention will be fulfilled in the future. Thus the Christian emphasis on, and confidence in, the new in the future is given a dual base: on the one hand, in the divine providence which brings in the new to each historical epoch— for providence is the basis of all eschatological promises that relate to the ongoing processes of history;[29] and, on the other, the newly challenged and empowered freedom of man who is to enact his humanity before God in responsibility in creating that new.

In sum, as religious symbols arise in the historical past, impinge in clarifying, illuminating, and healing thematization on the concrete present, so they point forward to a new facticity in the future, a new social and historical order.

If it be an "ahistorical Platonism" to ignore the historical aspect of religious symbols in past events, and a suprahistorical mysticism to transcend the factuality of the present in one's assessment of contemporary religious experience, it is surely equally "unbiblical" to make the eschatological reference to the future either abstract or other-worldly. The factual elements contained in the future referents of Christian symbols are borne by their moral, social, and political implications, by the relevance of these symbols to the actual and concrete political and social destiny of our common life. We are called not first to heaven, but to fashion a new earth as well—and the shape of that new earth is, or will be, as factual and actual when the promised future arises as was the past at one time.

As our third chapter indicated, one of the most significant functions of mythical language in a scientific culture is to thematize our understanding of the future and so of our destiny. More than in any other epoch, the future has become an object of confidence and hope or of foreboding and despair for modern man, a large part of the locus of whatever meaning he is to find in his past and his present. Modernity peers anxiously into its future, wondering what its technological, economic, political, and social shape will be; and in his darker midnight hours, like some chiliast or Millerite of old, modern man wonders if in fact there will be a future for him or for his children at all.

Thus among his most significant symbolic forms are those with which modern man comprehends the nature of historical passage into the future, and so the forces that shape that future for good or for ill. Such comprehension is complex and subtle—and yet very significant: it involves an intelligible interrelating of the factors of a developing technology, changes in social structure, the unpredictable contours of political events, and the slower thorough-bass

developments of political and moral values, goals, and standards. All of these, in their varying ways, are incurably
"factual" in character, that is, they have to do with the concrete character of actuality in process, a character to be
known only by an empirical inquiry of the appropriate
nature. The historical destiny which man can partly understand and in small measure direct, but which always in the
end determines him, has its factual underside, and achievement of a relative freedom within history depends utterly
on man's comprehension of the concrete character of the
history in which he is immersed.[30]

As we argued, however, interlaced with these factual elements the predictability of which seems not impossible, are
the baffling interplay of forces which remain in large part
both mysterious to man and uncontrollable by him. Man's
intentional freedom to use his powers to create the "good"
is always intertwined with his bondage to self-interest; the
magnificent power of man to control all things is balanced
by his weakness in controlling himself; and always the
unpredictable river of historical time in which he is immersed bears him as it will. At best he can direct himself
on its course and within its bounds, but he cannot determine
the wider course of historical events themselves. Let us
recall how even the development and direction of technological change were quite beyond the control of "man";
technology has a fate of its own which bears us along
whether we will or no. Freedom in history, ambiguous as
it is, is always embedded in a destiny in which and on which
it works, but which it does not itself create or fully direct.

There are strange, heterogeneous components to historical passage: (a) the technological, social, and political destiny which carries man along, and which he can in part
know and deflect but never fully control; and (b) his own
intentionality, which he can in part realize, but the corrup-

tion and dissipation of which always turn out to be his most implacable and stubborn fate. These components mix together as the factors determining historical passage into the future, and thus is the comprehension of that passage inevitably made a theme for mythical explication. Inescapably these factual elements combine with an accompanying transcendent factor, represented on the nether side by the mystery and ambiguity of our freedom and on the hither side by the ultimate horizon or context of process as a whole within which history enacts itself. Thus, however "secular" may be the way in which a scientific culture seeks to understand its past and present, though such secularity of comprehension is never total, such a culture inevitably uses mythical language in understanding its own future destiny.

If this be so, then one of the most crucial roles for theology is the intelligible explication of the ways in which our passage into the future is to be comprehended—for reflection on the mythical discourse of its relevant community is the task of theology. The temptation of traditional theology at this point is to remain safely pious and to concentrate solely on the inherited symbols concerning the future as themselves exhaustively explicative of our destiny. Thus, much of the current "theology of the future" speaks *only* of the Biblical view of God, time, and the future; it bases its understanding of what is to come *only* on the implications of sacred events in the past; and it calculates the direction and shape of our future, and so of our responsibilities to it, *only* on the grounds of the divine promises recorded in scripture. The result is that again the factual element is lost.[31] For the fundamental purpose of Christian symbolism is to express the entrance of the God creatively into the concrete stuff of creation and hence of history, illustrated paradigmatically in the Incarnation. Thus, as Jesus' humanity is crucial to our understanding of him, so correspondingly the level of "secondary causality" is crucial to any theological understanding of how the future comes to be out of the present.

The theological interpretation of our destiny must include an understanding of the concrete and factual factors of technological, social, and political change as well as a delineation of the characteristic shape of the divine promises—else our symbolic modes of comprehension lose not only their experiential meaning but also their Biblical character entirely. As historical inquiry must be included in any theological comprehension of the *past* "mighty acts of God," lest, for example, we portray a docetic Christ; and as a phenomenological analysis of our ordinary experience is necessary for an understanding of the present existential meaning of religious symbols for us; so a cultural, social, and political analysis of the "secular" factors shaping the future is required if we are to understand Christianly our promised destiny. Theologically this means that eschatological symbols must be joined to the symbol of providence if we are to make Biblical sense of God's promises; and even more it means that Biblical and theological studies must be accompanied by disciplines illuminative of our concrete social history and of the movement of the present into the future.

Modernity has, therefore, changed but by no means eradicated either the necessity for myth or the fundamental forms of its discourse. Scientific understanding through disciplined inquiry of the spatiotemporal continuum in which we live has effected the transformation. It has exorcised the older form of the factual and, at first blush, seemed to separate religious language and thus theology from any relation to concrete actuality at all. But a deeper look at the situation of a scientific culture reveals a strange continuity. First of all, the actuality of scientific inquiry itself, perhaps the major new element in the historical character of our cultural life, reveals itself as merely the concrete cognitive manifestation of a deep experience of the divine Logos. Secondly, the mystery of passage and of freedom, of intentions and of bondage, of the anxiety and the promise of the impinging future, remain as unclarified for us as for any age—and this unclarity must be illuminated by religious discourse if we are to live with understanding, courage, and confidence. Thus does the concrete character of our culture require myth and theology in the new situation as in the old.

The forms, however, of the factual referents of mythical language have changed. The locus of the factual has shifted from an exclusive concentration on reports of wondrous events in the past. In the place of such reports has appeared, first, historical inquiry into the events originative of a community's life, secondly, phenomenological analysis of the character of ordinary, secular experience, and finally, social analysis of the historical factors determinative of our common future. Without these "factual" elements religious myth is as empty and rootless—and so meaningless—as were the ancient myths when they were stripped of their stories set in special times and places. But correspondingly, without the transcendent dimensions introduced by religious myths a culture cognizant merely of the factual will understand neither itself nor its destiny. For the shape of "the factual" it believes it understands, and the way it understands its future, will in the end be determined by its own unexamined myths. And such myths, because they are neither factual nor ideal, will fail either to calm its deepest anxieties or to ground its most important hopes.

Notes

CHAPTER I. **The Influence of Science on Recent Theology**

1. Cf. Godfrey Lienhardt, *Divinity and Experience* (Oxford: Clarendon Press, 1967), esp. Chapter 5, "The Myths of the Spear-Masters." The long involved story of Agothyothik's exploits in tricking Longar, conquering him and thus gaining the fishing spears for his people, as Lienhardt relates it, is directly in *historical* language, although its *content* concerns the establishment of the basic structures of the given world, both cultural and political, of the Dinka. To this writer, the best collection of myths of genesis, both of nature and of culture, for the two are not differentiated in most myths, is Charles Long's *Alpha: The Myths of Creation* (New York: George Braziller, 1963). In all of these the language is directly historical and factual, the content having to do with the establishment of the realm of history and of fact; cf., e.g., the Navaho and Pueblo myths, pp. 53–58, the Polynesian myth, pp. 91–98, and the Zuni myths, pp. 101–4. In each of these phenomenal language is used to describe transphenomenal events and actions. This "time that is no time," i.e., the time of creation and thus a time that transcends concrete time, is what Eliade calls "mythical time," and perhaps this is the best description of this strange context of myth, spoken about in phenomenal language and yet transcendent to the profane time of ordinary temporal sequence in the present. Cf. Mircea Eliade, *Cosmos and History* (New York: Harper Torchbooks, 1959), Chapters One and Two, esp. pp. 20–22. In any case, whatever the relation of mythical to profane time in primitive and ancient culture—and that precise relation would be difficult to uncover—in our own tradition, which is our subject now, the two were assumed to be continuous with one another so that if we went far enough back in profane time we would arrive at the time of the patriarchs, Noah, Adam and creation.

In sum, Bultmann's famous definition of myth is in so far accurate: "Myth speaks of the power or the powers which man supposes he experiences as the ground and limit of his world and of his own activity and suffering. He describes these powers in terms derived from the visible world, with its tangible objects and forces, and from human life, with its feelings, motives and potentialities. . . . He speaks of the other world in terms of this world, and of the gods in terms derived from human life." Rudolf Bultmann, "New Testament and Mythology," in *Kerygma and Myth*, ed. by H. W. Bartsch, tr. by R. H. Fuller (London: SPCK, 1953), p. 10. Our quarrel with Bultmann on myth is that (a) he recognizes as the referent of the word myth only a primitive, literalistic, univocal language which identifies its meaning with supernatural interventions, with sacred matters of fact. Thus Bultmann does not conceive of the current, sophisticated, analogical mode of religious and theological speech about God as myth, i.e., he fails to recognize the history of the development of mythical language which we are now tracing. Consequently (b) he quite overlooks the fact that his own mode of speaking about God, whenever he does so, is itself mythical—even by his own definition. For he speaks of "divine acts," "divine speaking," the divine "confronting us," etc., all of which is to describe the transcendent in terms derived from human life.

2. This is, of course, a familiar theme for students of Scripture. No one, however, has stated it more forcefully than G. E. Wright, who declares not only that Christian confession and so theology are essentially narration, but that, as opposed to ancient myth with its mythical time, Christian narration is a story of events in actual past history: "Christianity has always taught that in a real history of what once happened in the ancient world, God came and revealed himself. Hence the Bible presents factual history in which is seen the work of the living God." G. Ernest Wright and Reginald H. Fuller, *The Book of the Acts of God* (Garden City, N.Y.: Doubleday, 1957), p. 16. And "In other words, when biblical man confessed his faith, he did so by telling the story of his past, interpreted by his faith. He learned to present his faith in the form of history." *Ibid.*, p. 21.

3. In and around their discussions of the figure of Adam, Christian theologians have built most of their concepts concerning human nature, its powers, possibilities, and problems. Thus in developing this doctrine, philosophical, religious, and factual elements were merged without question and probably without conscious awareness. What is to be noted in all of the following is the way, unique to this tradition, that "ontological" structures characteristic of man are in many cases affirmed to be rooted in historical or "ontic" events and thus treated merely as historical "fact."

Perhaps, with Origen, the most creative and profound of the early fathers, Irenaeus (born circa 130 A.D.) in the following shows a sensitive but patient literalism: And he [Adam] would no doubt have retained this clothing [scratchy fig-leaves] ... if God ... had not clothed them with tunics of skins instead of fig-leaves. For this purpose, too, He interrogates them, that the blame might light upon the woman; and again, He interrogates her, that she might convey the blame to the serpent ... wherefore also He drove him out of Paradise, and removed him from the tree of Life, not because He envied him the tree of life, as some venture to assert, but because He pitied him, [and did not desire] that he should continue a sinner forever, nor that the sin which surrounded him should be immortal, and evil interminable and irremediable. But He set a bound to his [state of] sin, by interposing death, and thus causing sin to cease . . . so that man, ceasing at length to live in sin, and dying to it, might begin to live to God." Irenaeus, *Against Heresies*, Book III, Chapter XXIII, Sections 5 and 6, found in *The Ante-Nicene Fathers* (Grand Rapids: William B. Eerdmans, 1950), Vol. I, p. 457.

And from Augustine a confident statement as to how, and in what numbers, the human race had its origin: "Now that we have solved, as well as we could, this very difficult question about the eternal God creating new things, without any novelty of will, it is easy to see how much better it is that God was pleased to produce the human race from the one individual whom He created, than if He had originated it in several men. . . . And therefore God created only one single man, not, certainly, that he might be a solitary, bereft of all society, but that by this means the unity of society and the bond of concord might be more effectually commended to him, men being bound together not only by similarity of nature, but by family affection." *The City of God*, Book XII, Chapter XXI, found in *Basic Writings of St. Augustine*, ed. by Whitney J. Oates (New York: Random House, 1948), Vol. II, pp. 203–4.

The whole discussion in Thomas of the origin of the world (*ST*, I, Q. 46) and the origin of man includes symbolic, philosophical, and factual elements, the latter in principle based on revelation (See *ST*, I, Q. 46, Art. 2); the following, dealing with the "when" of the creation of the soul of Adam, is a typical example: "Therefore, if we admit the opinion of Augustine about the work of the six days, we may say that the human soul preceded in the work of the six days according to a certain generic likeness, so far as it has intellectual nature in common with the angels; but it was itself created at the same time as the body. According to other saints, however, both the body and the soul of the first man were produced in the work of the six days." *Summa Theologica*, I, Q. 90, Art. 4 (cf. also Qs. 91–102). *Basic Writings of St. Thomas Aquinas*, ed. by Anton C. Pegis (New York: Random House, 1944), Vol. I, p. 869.

And Calvin assumes the same fundamental "factuality" to his theological account of the beginning of the human race; let us note, as an aside, the typically existential concern of Calvin and his surprising —in comparison to Thomas—dualistic viewpoint: "And first let it be understood, that, by his being made of earth and clay, a restraint was laid upon pride; since nothing is more absurd than for creatures to glory in their excellence, who not only inhabit a cottage of clay, but who are themselves composed partly of dirt and dust and ashes. But as God not only deigned to animate the earthern [sic] vessel, but chose to make it the residence of an immortal spirit, Adam might justly glory in so great an instance of the liberality of his Maker.

"That man consists of soul and body, ought not to be controverted. By the 'soul' I understand an immortal, yet created essence, which is the nobler part of him." John Calvin, *Institutes of the Christian Religion*, tr. by John Allen (Philadelphia: Presbyterian Board of Christian Education, 1930), Vol. I, Book I, Chapter XV, Sections 1 and 2, p. 203.

4. Reference is here made to the article entitled "Theological Reflexions on Monogenism," in Karl Rahner, *Theological Investigations,* tr. by Cornelius Ernst, O.P. (London: Darton, Longman and Todd, 1961), Vol. I, pp. 229–96. In this article Rahner tries to assess whether this doctrine (that the human race begins with one man and one pair) is (a) *directly* probable, certain, absolutely indispensable, etc. in tradition, in Scripture, in encyclicals, and so on, and (b) whether it is *indirectly* implied in other directly binding doctrines (e.g., that of original sin). In the process he enunciates the following interesting principle directly relevant to our present discussion: "It is utterly unacceptable from the viewpoint of Catholic theology to regard some object (or the inquiry into it) as dogmatically or theologically irrelevant just because it is also to be found in the field of the profane sciences or has such a scientific aspect or consequence" (p. 274). That is to say, if it has on its own grounds good reasons for asserting a matter of fact, dogmatic theology must regard itself as able and bound so to do. Thus on the same ground as that propounded by Augustine (n. 3 above), Rahner concludes that there was in fact one pair from which the human race has descended: "Scripture knows of such a common situation of salvation and ruin only in so far as men are of one stock" (p. 279). His main argument, however, is that original sin, as a necessary doctrine of Christianity, is "inconceivable" unless it concerns the act of one parental pair which are the sole progenitors for all men, i.e., that this doctrine no longer will rationally *explain* sin (as well as symbolize it) if it does not refer to (a) a historical act, (b) to an act of a particular and so single pair, (c) and be the act of the original pair (pp. 279–84).

In all of this Rahner shows that on this point (whether we can assert matters of fact on dogmatic grounds) he was at this stage "pre-modern," and thus did not yet reflect the immense pressures of modernity which we have cited in the text. It is by no means irrelevant that subsequently he has modified this position, and has in fact been followed in it by no important "liberal" Catholic theologians.

5. "The other three rivers [Moses] mentions only briefly by name. Gihon is the Nile, which flows through Egypt and encompasses the land of Ethiopia. Hiddekel is the very swift river Tigris, and the fourth is the Euphrates. Thus [Moses] describes the Garden of Eden, which has been lost by sin. Of it there remain only the four rivers, though these, too, have been changed, first by sin and then by the Flood" (Gen. 2:13, 14). *Luther's Commentary on Genesis,* tr. by J. Theodore Mueller (Grand Rapids: Zondervan, 1958), Vol. I, p. 50.

6. Cf. Charles C. Gillispie, *Genesis and Geology* (New York: Harper Torchbooks, 1959). "He [The Rev. David Scot] was particularly concerned with identifying the Saphan, a beast mentioned in Leviticus 11:5; Deuteronomy 14:7, Psalm 104:18, and Proverbs 30:26" (p. 71). My debt to Professor Gillispie's interesting and learned study will be evident throughout this chapter.

7. It was characteristic of most deist literature to scorn the need for and even the possibility of special divine acts of revelation during the course of historical time in favor of a universal, changeless, and

so timeless "natural religion" characteristic of all men and all places. However, the content of natural religion included as its main tenets the affirmation of divine, and so at least "unique," activity at the beginning and the end of the temporal process, affirmations which a subsequent naturalistic empiricism (in the figure of David Hume) was later to remove as themselves irrational. For examples of deism on this point, cf. Lord Herbert of Cherbury, *De Veritate*, esp. Chapters X and XI; John Toland, *Christianity Not Mysterious*, Chapter II (here revelation reveals "matters of fact" unknowable by natural reason, but important for our salvation, such as Creation and the Last Judgment); and Matthew Tindal, *Christianity As Old As Creation*. Relevant excerpts from these may be found in Peter Gay, ed., *Deism: An Anthology* (Princeton: D. Van Nostrand, 1968).

8. For an expression of this assumption (that the revealed doctrine of Creation sets the basic framework for scientific understanding), cf. the eminent John Ray (1627–1705), one of the founders of the Royal Society and also of modern biology, in his *The Wisdom of God Manifested in the Works of the Creation*: The works of the Creation, said Ray, were "the Works created by God at first, and by Him conserved to this Day in the same State and Condition in which they were first made"; and these notions, says historian John C. Greene, "defined the human situation, the purpose of science, the means of knowledge, the basis of social obligation, the relations between nature, man, and God." John C. Greene, *The Death of Adam* (Ames: Iowa State University Press, 1959), p. 5. The same point was made by the eighteenth-century Dutch mathematician and physicist, W. J. S. Gravesande: "Physics do not meddle with the first Formation of Things. That the World was created by God is a Position wherein Reason so perfectly agrees with Scripture, that the least Examination of Nature will show plain Footsteps of Supreme Wisdom." W. J. S. Gravesande, *Mathematical Elements of Natural Philosophy*, I, ix, quoted in Gillispie, *op. cit.*, p. 12.

The certainty with which the European world, until the nineteenth century, took this Biblical picture of a recent Creation and of a certain number of fixed species, is well illustrated by the two following comments, the first from Sir Thomas Browne in 1635, and the second from Thomas Jefferson in 1785: " 'Time we may comprehend,' wrote Sir Thomas Browne in the *Religio Medici*, ' 'tis but five days elder than ourselves, and hath the same horoscope with the World' " (quoted in Loren Eiseley, *Darwin's Century* [Garden City, N.Y.: Doubleday, 1959], p. 2). And from Jefferson: "Such is the economy of nature that no instance can be produced of her having permitted any one race of her animals to become extinct" (quoted in Greene, *op. cit.*, p. 88).

The entire historical account in this chapter of the relation of Enlightenment science to revealed doctrine is vastly indebted to these works of Professors Gillispie, Greene, and Eiseley, as well as to Ian Barbour's *Issues in Science and Religion* (Englewood Cliffs, N.J.: Prentice-Hall, 1966).

9. In most of his writing on religion, Immanuel Kant reflects a

thoroughly moralized (and so modernized) as opposed to a factual-informative view of revelation. Nevertheless, even in his case, some of the older assumptions about the authority of Scripture vis-à-vis the Beginning sometimes reappeared, as in the following surprising remark in a footnote in his *Religion Within the Limits of Reason Alone*: "In any case, the sacred books of this people [the Jews] will doubtless always be preserved and will continue to possess value for scholarship even if not for the benefit of religion: since the history of no other people dates back, with some color of credibility, so far as does this, into epochs of antiquity (even to the beginning of the world [*sic*]) in which all secular history known to us can be arranged; and thus the great hiatus, which must be left by the latter, is filled by the former." *Op. cit.*, tr. by T. M. Greene and H. H. Hudson (New York: Harper Torchbooks, 1960), Book Four, Part One, Section Two, p. 154, footnote. How the formulator of the nebular hypothesis could have so regarded the Scriptural time scale remains a mystery to this writer!

10. Cf. Bacon's influential definition of Natural Theology: ". . . that spark of knowledge of God which may be had by the light of nature and the consideration of created things: and thus can fairly be held to be *divine* in respect of its object, and *natural* in respect of its source of information." Quoted in Clement C. J. Webb, *Studies in the History of Natural Theology* (Oxford: Clarendon Press, 1915), p. 2.

For an instructive example of the distinction of natural and revealed theology, as interpreted by a distinguished scientist and devout believer of the eighteenth century, cf. the following from Joseph Priestley: "With respect to both natural and revealed religion, all that we have to do is to consider whether *actual appearances* and known *facts* can be accounted for on any other hypothesis. In natural religion the appearances to be accounted for are *the constitution and laws of nature*. In revealed religion, they are certain *historical facts*, as indisputable as any natural appearances. They are the belief of the miracles of Moses and Christ, and that of his resurrection, in given circumstances." Joseph Priestley, *Letters to a Philosophic Unbeliever*, I, pp. 176–177, quoted in Gillispie, *op. cit.*, pp. 33–34. (Italics in the original.) Let us note especially how for Priestley revealed religion deals with *facts* as the almost exclusive data relevant to its message.

11. One of the best literary examples of this sense that nature in all her beauty and harmony proclaims her divine author is Joseph Addison's (1672–1719) familiar hymn; let us note how the second of these two verses reflects some of the terror felt at the cold nonsensate character of the harmonious world that the new science had then just uncovered, and that we can now vividly see, not only in Kubric's film *2001*, but live on television in our own living rooms!

> The spacious firmament on high
> With all the blue ethereal sky
> And spangled heav'ns, a shining frame
> Their great Original proclaim;

Th' unwearied sun, from day to day,
Does his Creator's power display,
And publishes to every land
The work of an almighty hand.

What tho' in solemn silence all
Move round the dark terrestrial ball?
What tho' no real voice nor sound
Amid the radiant orbs be found?
In reason's ear they all rejoice,
And utter forth a glorious voice;
For ever singing, as they shine,
"The hand that made us is divine."

12. Cf. the position represented by the "natural religionists" or deists from Lord Herbert in the early seventeenth century on roughly to Kant in the late eighteenth, that no "special revelation" through the Word was either necessary or useful in religion, since all that was essential to salvation, if God be just, must be universally knowable by all through nature or conscience. All that the more "conservative" defenders of relevation, from John Locke to Toland, could argue was that revelation was (a) not irrational, and (b) that it presented us with knowledge of significant "facts" not ascertainable from nature. For illustrations of this debate, cf. John Locke, *The Reasonableness of Christianity*, and John Toland, *Christianity Not Mysterious*. An excellent survey of this debate is J. M. Creed and J. S. B. Smith, *Religious Thought in the Eighteenth Century* (Cambridge: University Press, 1934).

13. For example, see the following from John Calvin, the ultimate source of much of the theology dominant in the minds of many early English scientists: "It must therefore be confessed, that in each of the works of God, but more especially in the whole considered together, there is a bright exhibition of the divine perfections: by which the whole human race is invited and allured to the knowledge of God, and thence to true and complete felicity." "Yet they [our Biblical references] will all tend to prove, that the Scripture discovers God to us as the Creator of the world, and declares what sentiments we should form of him, that we may not be seeking after a deity in the labyrinth of uncertainty." ". . . The Scripture distinguishes the only true God by certain characters and titles, as the Creator and Governor of the world, that he may not be confounded with the multitude of false gods. Therefore, though every man should seriously apply himself to a consideration of the works of God, being placed in this very splendid theatre to be a spectator of them, yet he ought principally to attend to the word, that he may attain superior advantages." *Institutes* Book I, Chapter V, Section X, p. 73, and Chapter VI, Sections I and II, pp. 81–82.

14. Cf. John C. Greene, *op. cit.*, esp. pp. 129–37. After his own summary, Greene quotes Ray (1627–1705) as follows: "Science and

religion were in perfect accord, 'the number of species being in nature certain and determinate, as is generally acknowledged by philosophers, and might be proved also by divine authority, God having finished his works of creation, that is, consummated the number of species in six days'" (p. 131). Commenting on Linnaeus (1707–1778), Greene says, "In his *Philosophia botanica* he defined species as primordial types created by divine wisdom and perpetuated by generation from the beginning to the end of the world" (p. 133).

15. The close connection or rather parallel in the mind of the "catastrophists" between *Heilsgeschichte* and the tumultuous events of the early geological history of the earth is illustrated by the following from the Rev. Joseph Townsend in his book entitled *The Character of Moses Established for Veracity as an Historian, Recording Events from the Creation to the Deluge* (1813): "The science of geology becomes of infinite importance, when we consider it as connected with our immortal hopes. These depend upon the truth of revelation, and the whole system of revealed religion is ultimately connected with the veracity of Moses.

"The divine legation of Christ, and of the Jewish Lawgivers, must stand or fall together. If the Mosaic account of the creation and of the deluge is true, and consequently the promises recorded by him well founded, we may retain our hopes; but should the former be given up as false, we must renounce the latter." Vol. I, p. 430. Quoted in Gillispie, *op. cit.*, p. 94.

16. Georges Cuvier, *Essay on the Theory of the Earth* . . . (First American Edition, New York, 1818), p. 44. Quoted in Greene, *op. cit.*, p. 124.

17. William Buckland, *Vindicae Geologicae; or the Connexion of Geology with Religion Explained* (Oxford, 1820), quoted in Gillispie, *op. cit.*, p. 103.

18. For an early example of the assumed continuity between Biblical time, Biblical stories, and Biblical facts on the one hand, and the events and facts to be uncovered by "secular history" on the other, cf. the following title page: "*The History of the World in Five Books*, by Sir Walter Ralegh [sic] Knight, London, printed for Tho. Basset, Ric. Chiswell, Benj. Tooke, Tho. Passenger, Geo. Dawes, Tho. Sawbridge, M. Wooton, and G. Conyers, 1687. The First, Intreating of the Beginning and First Ages of the same, from the Creation unto Abraham. The Second, Of the Times from the Birth of Abraham to the Destruction of the Temple of Solomon."

19. Charles Lyell, *Principles of Geology* (London, 1830–33), Vol. I, p. 144, quoted in Gillispie, *op. cit.*, p. 126.

20. The similarity of this basic methodological principle of uniformitarianism in geology (i.e., that all laws used to explain the *past* are to be found operating in *current* experience) to the corresponding "principle of analogy" basic to historical explanation as formulated by Ernst Troeltsch some seventy-five years later, is striking of the congruence, for all their obvious differences, between the naturalistic explanations of physical events and the naturalistic-humanistic ex-

planations of historical events. For a very valuable contemporary discussion of Troeltsch's principles of historical inquiry, cf. Van A. Harvey, *The Historian and the Believer* (New York: The Macmillan Company, 1966), Chapter I.

21. Gillispie, *op. cit.*, pp. 130–35, 221.

22. Cf. Paul Tillich, *Systematic Theology* (Chicago: University of Chicago Press, 1951), Vol. 1, pp. 80–86, 110; Vol. II, pp. 37–38, 151–52; *The Theology of Culture* (New York: Oxford University Press, 1959), Chapter V, "The Nature of Religious Language"; *The Dynamics of Faith* (New York: Harper Torchbooks, 1957), Chapter III. "The Symbols of Faith," and Chapter V, "The Truth of Faith," esp. pp. 50–54 and 80–89. For Reinhold Niebuhr's elucidation of a similar distinction between "primitive" and "permanent" myth, cf. the article "The Truth in Myths" in *The Nature of Religious Experience*, ed. J. S. Bixler (New York: Harper & Brothers, 1937), and the sermon "As Deceivers Yet True," in *Beyond Tragedy* (New York: Charles Scribner's Sons, 1937).

23. Paul Ricoeur has insisted that in contemporary life myth is both essential for the fullness of language and so of understanding, and yet must be taken, not as giving us an explanation of the historical or factual causes of things, but as opening to us their deeper, transcendent dimensions. Cf. *The Symbolism of Evil* (New York: Harper & Row, 1967), esp. pp. 161–64, and 232–43.

24. Cf. the author's *Naming the Whirlwind: The Renewal of God Language* (Indianapolis: Bobbs-Merrill, 1969), for a more extended discussion of the meaning of religious language in a secular culture.

25. On this point, cf. Ian Barbour, *op. cit.*, esp. pp. 35, 156 f., 162, and 284. Barbour says, ". . . Until this century most scientists assumed a simple realism in which theories were conceived as exact replicas of the world" (p. 162). Cf. also the confirmation of this in the very interesting article on models, scientific and theological, by Frederick Ferré, "Mapping the Logic of Models in Science and Theology," in Dallas High, *New Essays on Religious Language* (New York: Oxford University Press, 1969), pp. 54–96.

26. For a vivid portrayal of the anxiety of soul of educated Christians in the nineteenth century due to the changes of *Weltanschauung* issued in by science, cf. Basil Willey, *Nineteenth Century Studies* (London: Chatto & Windus, 1950), esp. Chapters VIII–X. As Matthew Arnold described his age (which to us seems so serene and confident!): "An iron time of doubts, disputes, distractions, fears" and "between two worlds, one dead, the other powerless to be born" (*op. cit.*, pp. 252–53). As Willey makes clear, the cause of the doubts, fears, and death in these remarks was not so much war and social unrest, as in our own age, as it was the utter uncertainty the age felt about the certainties of faith on which that "Christian civilization" had been built.

27. Cf. Ludwig Feuerbach, *Lectures on the Essence of Religion*, tr. by Ralph Manheim (New York: Harper & Row, 1967), esp. pp. 194–98, 202–6, 207–9, 232–34; and *The Essence of Christianity*, tr. by

George Eliot (New York: Harper Torchbooks, 1957), esp. Chapter I, Section II, "The Essence of Religion."

28. Reference is here made to the intense debate in the philosophy of the twentieth century over whether philosophy is, as it was classically understood to be, a way of *knowing* reality through speculative thought, "the really real," "the actual," "the concrete" and so on; or whether, not being a way of knowing at all, it is more modestly a mode of analysis and clarification of the kinds of language men use in their various "forms of life." For this change cf. G. J. Warnock, *English Philosophy Since 1900* (London: Oxford University Press, 1958); J. O. Urmson, *Philosophical Analysis: Its Development Between the Two World Wars* (Oxford: Clarendon Press, 1960); and Richard Rorty, *The Linguistic Turn* (Chicago: University of Chicago Press, 1967).

29. The unity of evolution and theism in liberal Christianity is well illustrated by many post-Darwinian theologians. No one celebrated this surprising marriage more fervently than Lyman Abbott, as the following indicates: "Evolution is described by John Fiske as 'God's way of doing things.' Theology also may be described as an attempt to explain God's way of doing things. Thus, to a certain extent, the science of evolution and the science of theology have the same ultimate end." And, "I reverently and heartily accept the axiom of theology that a personal God is the foundation of all life; but I also believe that God has but one way of doing things; that His way may be described in one word as the way of growth, or development, or evolution, terms which are substantially synonymous; that He resides in the world of nature and in the world of man; that there are no laws of nature which are not the laws of God's own being; that there are no forces of nature, that there is only one divine, infinite force, always proceeding from, always subject to the will of God; that there are not occasional or exceptional theophanies, but that all nature and all life is one great theophany; that there are not occasional interventions in the order of life which bear witness to the presence of God, but that life is itself a perpetual witness to His presence. . . . In so far as the theologian and evolutionist differ in their interpretation of the history of life . . . I agree with the evolutionist, not with the theologian." Lyman Abbott, *The Theology of an Evolutionist* (Boston: Houghton, Mifflin, 1897), pp. 3–4, 9–10. On the same theme cf. also Lyman Abbott, *Evolution of Christianity* (Boston: Houghton, Mifflin, 1892), pp. 2f., 254–55; Henry Drummond, *Natural Law in the Spiritual World* (New York: J. Pott & Company, 1884), pp. 212–19, 281; and *The Ascent of Man* (London: Hodder & Stoughton, 1894), pp. 11–12, 52–53, 427, 438, and 441–44.

30. The reference here is to Calvin's vivid analogy: "For, as persons who are old, or whose eyes are by any means become dim, if you show them the most beautiful book, though they perceive something written but can scarcely read two words together, yet, by the assistance of spectacles, will begin to read distinctly,—so the Scripture, collecting in our minds the otherwise confused notions of Deity, dispels the

darkness, and gives us a clear view of the true God." *Institutes*, Book I, Chapter VI, Section I, p. 80.

31. Perhaps the most striking example of this disjunction between the *Historie* of which the historian speaks, and the *Geschichte* of which the theologian speaks, is in Barth's distinction between the *Urgeschichte* of God with which revelation is concerned, and the ordinary history of everyday life with which secular history is concerned. For example, the following from the *Römerbrief*: "Over all historical possibilities and probabilities and necessities and certainties death is supreme, for they all are mortal and passing to corruption. Were there a direct and causal connexion between the historical 'facts' of the Resurrection—the empty tomb, for example, or the appearances detailed in 1st Corinthians XV—and the Resurrection itself; were it in any sense of the word a 'fact' in history, then no profession of faith or refinement of devotion could prevent it being involved in the see-saw of 'Yes' and 'No,' life and death, God and man, which is characteristic of all that happens on the historical plane. There is under this heaven and this earth no existence or occurrence, no transformation, be it never so striking, no experience, be it never so unique, no miracle, be it never so unheard of, which is not caught up by a relativity in which great and small are inextricably woven together. Therefore, if the Resurrection be brought within the context of history, it must share in its obscurity and error and essential questionableness." Karl Barth, *The Epistle to the Romans*, tr. from the 6th edition by Edwyn C. Hoskyns (London: Oxford University Press, 1933), p. 204. The influence of the modern conception of the relativity and temporality of all things in time, and so the impossibility of a direct or unequivocal manifestation of the Absolute in phenomena, is crystal clear in this exegetical passage, leading as it does to the sharp distinction between the history in which God acts, and the history about which mortals, unaided by grace, can speak.

32. This chapter is, of course, a studied criticism of certain aspects of this view of neo-orthodoxy. However, many critics of neo-orthodoxy are somewhat confused as to what is really amiss here. Ian Barbour, for example, who otherwise is the present dean of commentors on science and theology, roundly criticizes neo-orthodoxy for insisting on a separation between scientific hypotheses and the affirmations of theology, as if the separation or distinction between the two was the mistake. Cf. esp. his article "Science and Religion Today," in *Science and Religion*, Ian Barbour, ed. (New York: Harper & Row, 1968), esp. pp. 9–14. Surely this is to misunderstand the situation. His own mentor Whitehead distinguishes clearly between scientific hypotheses, religious truths and metaphysical truths, and would insist that metaphysical statements about the primordial nature of God are *not* continuous with statements in physics or biology. To be sure, developmental views derived from various special sciences have generated much of process philosophical and theological thought; nonetheless, it has only been when these scientific propositions have been *expanded out* of their scientific arena into propositions with universal

scope that statements of metaphysical or theological scope have appeared. Thus it is not the neo-orthodox separation of theological statements from scientific statements that bothers Barbour. For, in Barbour's own view, scientific and religious statements are not continuous but quite distinct; where he differs with the neo-orthodox is that he believes that there is a metaphysical level of statement higher than either which can mediate between them and which therefore can overcome the distinction. Thus the question of the possibility or viability of a metaphysical mediation between science and theology is the real issue here. Barbour believes in metaphysics; most of the neo-orthodox did not—but *that* is not to say they were wrong in making a quite different point, namely, an important distinction of levels of discourse between science and theology which Barbour himselm makes. Barbour also somewhat gratuitously assumes that all who view the distinction between science and theology in a neo-orthodox way are automatically uninterested in and scornful of ontology. In my own book on the issue of creation, *Maker of Heaven and Earth* (Garden City, N.Y.: Doubleday, 1959) I argue as cogently as I can that without a corresponding ontology a theological view of creation makes no sense, not least because there is then no resolution possible with science—but since the view of theology there represented was "neo-orthodox" and not Whiteheadian, Barbour apparently could not credit these passages!

The issue broached in this present chapter is of course a quite different one, namely, whether or not implications of science have affected the way theology understands its own truth, and here the interrelatedness of science and theology is, we feel, undeniable—although they remain different levels of discourse. Perhaps one could say that just as the Neo-orthodox made too simplistic a separation of science and theology, so the metaphysicians have made too simplistic a distinction between those who are of Whitehead and believe in interrelatedness, and those who are of Kierkegaard and apparently do not.

33. The influence of existentialism in developing this sense of a split between the understanding of natural objects and of man, and so correspondingly between nature and history, was immense. Perhaps the most extreme example of this split was the theological work of Carl Michalson, for whom the distinction of nature and of history represented a dichotomy equal almost to that of Sin and Grace, unbelief and faith. Cf. *The Rationality of Faith* (New York: Charles Scribner's Sons, 1963).

34. Cf. Immanuel Velikovsky, *Worlds in Collision* (Garden City, N.Y.: Doubleday, 1950).

35. The separation of "ordinary" knowledge of natural and historical events, and religious and theological knowledge of those events as "acts of God," was in neo-orthodoxy indeed sharp; and this distinction reappeared in countless forms. Cf. for example Emil Brunner's distinction between the *natural knowledge* that "expands the self," "gives it power," "isolates me from others," and "has no transforming effect," with *revelation* which judges and transforms the inward man

and establishes communion with God and others (*Revelation and Reason*, tr. by Olive Wyon [Philadelphia: Westminster Press, 1946], pp. 25–29); and thus only those who have personally encountered God through these events can see God there (*ibid.*, pp. 84–88, 114–30). Cf. also, for another version of this same theme, Karl Barth, *Church Dogmatics*, tr. T. H. L. Parker, *et al.* (Edinburgh: T. & T. Clark, 1957), Vol. II, Part I, Section XXVII, I, "The Hiddenness of God," pp. 179–204. Thus the events which faith affirms to be the mighty acts of God are, viewed by natural knowledge, indistinguishable from all natural and historical processes; cf. G. Ernest Wright, *The Books of the Act of God*, p. 18, and B. W. Anderson, *Understanding the Old Testament* (Englewood Cliffs, N.J.: Prentice-Hall, 1957), pp. 47–49. Cf. also Gustav Aulen, *The Faith of the Christian Church*, tr. by E. H. Wahlstrom and G. E. Arden (Philadelphia: Muhlenberg Press, 1948), esp. pp. 53–59.

36. That both of the great Reformers men were "precritical" in the sense that for them the Bible contains divinely revealed theological propositions which are not relative but eternal, not fallible or partial but utterly true—and thus proper exegesis can uncover these nonrelative and changeless truths—the following from Luther and Calvin respectively attest: "But a Christian knows that his teaching comes from God's inspiration and that it is true and right and perfect. This must not be taken to mean that a man's life is perfect and that he is calling his life 'innocent.' For we are all sinners and have no right to brag about our innocence. . . . Here, where His Word is, everything is clear and good, but concerning our life we dare not boast. Concerning our speech we should boast before God and men of our certainty that our teaching is correct. . . . This is evident from the fact that it builds upon the Lord Christ, it lets God be our Lord God, and it gives God the glory. This teaching is correct, and it cannot go wrong; nor will anyone improve on it." "Commentary on Psalm 26," *Luther's Works*, ed. by Jaroslav Pelikan (St. Louis: Concordia, 1955), Vol. XII, pp. 185–87.

And from Calvin, speaking of Scripture: "But since we are not favoured with daily oracles from heaven, and since it is only in the Scriptures that the Lord hath been pleased to preserve his truth in perpetual remembrance, it obtains the same complete credit and authority with believers, when they are satisfied of its divine origin, as if they heard the very words pronounced by God Himself." *Institutes*, Book I, Chapter VII, p. 85.

37. For examples of this vivid sense among modern Catholic theologians of the historical relativity of all our dogmatic statements, cf. the following from Karl Rahner: "Yet all human statements, even those in which faith expresses God's saving truths, are finite. By this we mean that they never declare the *whole* of the reality. In the last resort every reality, even the most limited, is connected with and related to every other reality." "But because our statements about the infinite realities are finite and in this sense inadequate—that is, while actually corresponding to reality, yet not simply congruent with

it—so every formula in which the faith is expressed can in principle be surpassed while still retaining its truth. That is to say, in principle at least it can be replaced by another which says the same thing." Karl Rahner, *Theological Investigations*, Vol. I, Chapter III, "The Development of Dogma," pp. 43–44.

And from E. Schillebeeckx: "The difference between the 'dogmatic essence' and its historical 'mode of expression' is therefore an unassailable datum, but it is also virtually meaningless and unmanageable, precisely because this 'essence' is never given to us as a pure essence, but is always concealed *in* a historical mode of expression. A partial affirmation *is*, after all, never completely true. No distinction can therefore be made in it between a completely true, unchangeable essence and changeable modes of expressing this essence —the absolute penetrates all relative interpretations, the one is never present without the other." "For we do not possess the absolute which acts as an inner norm to our faith in an absolute way; we possess it only within our historical situation." E. Schillebeeckx, *God the Future of Man*, tr. by N. D. Smith (New York: Sheed & Ward, 1968), pp. 12 and 39–40.

38. For a longer discussion of this problem in neo-orthodox theology, cf. *Naming the Whirlwind: The Renewal of God Language*, pp. 78–106, 190–202.

39. It is interesting that this same criticism of neo-orthodoxy as "too subjectivist," i.e., as locating the divine revelation in an "Epiphany" in which God Himself manifests Himself to the inward soul of man, is found brilliantly expressed in Wolfhart Pannenberg and Jürgen Moltmann. For the first, cf. the "Introduction" to *Revelation As History*, ed. Wolfhart Pannenberg (New York: Macmillan, 1968), and "The Revelation of God in Jesus of Nazareth" in *Theology as History*, ed. by James M. Robinson and John B. Cobb, Jr. (New York: Harper & Row, 1967); cf. also *Jesus: God and Man*, tr. by L. L. Wilkins and D. A. Priebe (Philadelphia: Westminster Press, 1968), pp. 127–33. For the same criticism in Moltmann, cf. *The Theology of Hope* (New York: Harper & Row, 1967), Chapter I.

The real methodological difficulty with this new eschatology of Pannenberg and Moltmann, in our view, is that (a) they accept the modern principles cited above concerning the relativity of all historical events to their surrounding context, and thus the necessity of a critical historical approach to such events (i.e., each of them *argues historically* for the validity of the appearances and so of the Resurrection, rather than merely accepting them as certainly "given" because of Scriptural assertions about them). (b) On the other hand, they reject the neo-orthodox answer to this problem, namely, that revelation is not an event on the plane of history available to ordinary knowledge, but rather the self-manifestation of God through relative events and propositions to the inwardness of man. In place of this, they put a concept of revelation as "objective history." But if the point of contact with God is not inward, it must be outward and thus objective. Thus a revelation which is proleptic of the future is driven

to locate such revelation in (a) the verbal promises enshrined in the
propositions of Scripture, and (b) in objective events which by their
visibly supernatural character bespeak the activity of God. Correspondingly, it follows that faith must follow *from* the knowledge of
these events as miraculous, rather than being the presupposition of
their knowledge (cf. Pannenberg, "The Revelation of God in Jesus
of Nazareth" in *Theology as History*, pp. 128–29, and "Dogmatic
Theses on the Doctrine of Revelation," in *Revelation as History*,
pp. 135 f.) This location of revelation in objective events in history
runs counter, however, to their *other* assumption of the relativity and
secularity of all historical events to the profane gaze of the historian. And so they must amend once more their view of revelation,
and admit that presupposed in the possibility of a resurrection event
is a "knowledge of God" and the acceptance of an Apocalyptic tradition
—which begin to look very much like what the neo-orthodox called
"faith." Cf. Pannenberg, "The Revelation of God in Jesus of Nazareth," pp. 109 f., and "Dogmatic Theses on the Doctrine of Revelation,"
pp. 145 f. Needless to say, this in turn contradicts or at least radically
qualifies the assertion above that knowledge of the Resurrection is
"natural knowledge" in that it precedes faith and so presupposes no
faith. Until this confusion is cleared up, it is difficult to know *what*
this theology is saying on this issue, as this summary sentence indicates: "The events in which God demonstrates his deity are *self-evident* as they stand within the framework of *their own history*,"
ibid., p. 155. (Italics added.)

The same ambiguities appear in Moltmann. For him, the Resurrection is a "historic" event to be known by reason and inquiry and
not by faith, for it is the foundation and not the result of faith (*op.
cit.*, pp. 172 f.) ; and it is the basis for belief in God as the God of
promise and faithfulness (*ibid.*, pp. 86 f., 145 f., 192 f.). On the other
hand, this event can be "known" only by one who has a special view
of history and its possibilities (pp. 174–75), one who believes in God
as Creator *ex nihilo* (p. 175) ; and it is "historic," not in that it fits
certain categories of historicity, but because it creates a history in
which man can live confidently (p. 181)—all of this presupposing
some sort of "faith stance" over against a "secular" stance.

40. Pannenberg interestingly traces the development of the neo-orthodox view of revelation as an Epiphany, that is, a self-manifestation of God in the present and to the inwardness of man, to Hegel,
then through Schleiermacher, and thence to Barth and Bultmann, a
stream of inheritance almost as surprising as Moltmann's remark
that the origin of the neo-orthodox view of God's presence lay in the
early Greek Parmenides! cf. Pannenberg, "Introduction," *Revelation
As History*, pp. 4–9; Moltmann, *op. cit.*, pp. 30–31, 40–42, 48 f.

41. For a more extended discussion of this point, see *Naming The
Whirlwind*, pp. 203–27.

42. The secular prophets or seers who look ahead into our culture's
future are apparently agreed that religious belief and with it any
organized religious practices will not be an important characteristic

of our future, if they will be there at all. Victor Ferkiss, reporting on this vision, says in a footnote: "So much is the decline of religion taken for granted that it is rarely mentioned." Victor Ferkiss, *Technological Man: The Myth and the Reality* (New York: George Braziller, 1969), p. 286. And Herman Kahn illustrates this by describing the culture toward which we are now moving as "sensate," i.e., "worldly, naturalistic, realistic, . . ." or "worldly, humanistic, or empirical." Herman Kahn and Anthony J. Wiener, "A Framework for Speculation," *Daedalus: Toward the Year 2000: Work in Progress*, Summer, 1967, Vol. 96, No. 3, pp. 706–8. Whether these predictions are in fact credible or not will be the subject of our next two chapters.

CHAPTER II.   **Religious Dimensions in Science**

1. For a fuller discussion of the meaning of secularity, cf. *Naming The Whirlwind*, Part I, Chapter 2.

2. Julian Huxley, *Religion Without Revelation*, new and rev. ed. (New York: Harper & Brothers, 1957). Teilhard de Chardin, *The Phenomenon of Man* (New York: Harper & Row, 1961); *The Divine Milieu* (New York: Harper & Row, 1960). Apparently Teilhard did not agree with the "out" I am here giving to him, for in his Preface to *The Phenomenon of Man*, he asserts that what is presented there is neither metaphysics nor theology (though it may "look like" the former) but "purely scientific reflections" which are moving toward philosophy and theology because they seek to picture the phenomenon of man as a whole (*ibid.*, pp. 29–30).

3. Huxley, *op. cit.*, esp. pp. 212–20.

4. Stephen Toulmin, "Contemporary Scientific Mythology," in *Metaphysical Beliefs*, ed. by A. Macintyre, (London: SCM Press, 1957), pp. 13–81.

5. As Frederick Ferré has put this point: "Just as theologians needed to learn that their statements of universal scope were not designed to rival the function of the scientist's limited and empirically confirmable propositions, so scientists require a warning against supposing that their carefully controlled and empirically specific statements could be set to work as propositions having unlimited scope and in competition with theology's—*while remaining scientific statements.* If a sentence bred in science's neatly fenced pasture wanders off to frolic in metaphysics' Elysian fields, it had better expect to receive new brand markings!" Frederick Ferré, "Mapping the Logic of Models in Science and Theology," in Dallas High, ed., *New Essays on Religious Language* (New York: Oxford University Press, 1969), p. 94. (Italics in the original.)

6. Charles C. Gillispie, *Genesis and Geology* (New York, Harper Torchbooks, 1959). John C. Greene, *The Death of Adam* (Ames: Iowa State University Press, 1959). Thomas Kuhn, *The Structure of Scientific Revolutions* (Chicago: University of Chicago Press, 1962). Stephen Toulmin, *Foresight and Understanding* (New York: Harper Torchbooks, 1961). Michael Polanyi, *Personal Knowledge* (New York: Harper Torchbooks, 1964); *The Tacit Dimension* (Garden City, N.Y.:

Doubleday Anchor, 1966); *Science, Faith and Society* (Chicago: University of Chicago Press, 1964). Bernard J. F. Lonergan, *Insight* (London: Longmans, 1964). Karl Rahner, *Hörer des Wortes* (München: Kösel-Verlag, 1963); *Spirit in the World*, tr. William Dych (New York: Herder & Herder, 1968). Paul Tillich, esp. *Das System der Wissenschaften nach Gegenständen und Methoden* (Göttingen: Vandenhoeck und Ruprecht, 1923); *My Search for Absolutes* (New York: Simon & Schuster, 1967). For a vigorous counterargument, cf. Israel Scheffler, *Science and Subjectivity* (Indianapolis: Bobbs-Merrill, 1967).

7. Cf., for example, the discussion of this issue in Dudley Shapere, *Philosophical Problems of Natural Science* (New York: The Macmillan Company, 1965), pp. 9–15. Cf. the following as examples of the logical analysis of science: R. B. Braithwaite, *Scientific Explanation* (Cambridge: University Press, 1953). Ernst Nagel, *The Structure of Science* (New York: Harcourt, Brace, 1961). Karl R. Popper, *The Logic of Scientific Discovery* (New York: Basic Books, 1959). Israel Scheffler, *The Anatomy of Inquiry* (New York: Alfred A. Knopf, 1963).

8. Cf. Shapere's "Introduction" to his book of readings in contemporary philosophy of science, (*op. cit.*, pp. 1–29). In this he outlines vividly and frankly the wide range of disagreement and even bafflement *vis-à-vis* the fundamental structure of science. The nature of the scientific method itself, the status of its theoretical terms, how testing of hypotheses takes place (or even if it does!), the linguistic or philosophical status of a scientific theory or a law, all seem to remain "mysteries" to the community of philosophers of science. A perusal of the relevant literature but confirms this summary. Ironically, while practicing scientists seem tacitly to possess common assumptions about science, its procedures, aims, and capabilities—and thus see no "mysteries" here at all—those who *reflect* on science seem unable to reach any clarity, much less agreement, on what these tacit structures of the scientific enterprise are.

9. Kuhn, *op. cit.*, pp. 92–93, 108–9, 150. Toulmin, *Foresight and Understanding*, p. 57. Polanyi, *Personal Knowledge*, pp. 150–60.

10. Again the philosopher Frederick Ferré is in agreement: "And even the most carefully run experiments by respected professionals are suspect if they purport to falsify well-established laws. Other beliefs will be abandoned, if necessary, much sooner. And the basic principles of a science *will not be verifiable or falsifiable at all*, in any straightforward sense, within the science itself. The vindication of a science's basic principles will be in the success of the science as a whole." Frederick Ferré, "Science and the Death of 'God,'" in Ian G. Barbour, ed., *Science and Religion* (New York: Harper & Row, 1968), pp. 138–39. (Italics in the original.)

11. Kuhn, *op. cit.*, pp. 95–96, 102, 108–9, 121, 125. Toulmin, *op. cit.*, pp. 44–59. Polanyi, *op. cit.*, pp. 166–170.

12. Kuhn, *op. cit.*, Chapter VIII, "The Response to Crisis," and IX, "The Nature and Necessity of Scientific Revolutions."

13. Cf. Toulmin, *op. cit.*, pp. 50–59. Polanyi, *op. cit.*, pp. 152–53.

14 A. N. Whitehead, *Modes of Thought* (New York: The Macmillan Company, 1956), pp. 66–67; cf. also *Adventures of Ideas* (New York: The Macmillan Company, 1933), p. 379.

15. Cf. Augustine, *On Free Will*: "Just as the rules of numbers are true and unchangeable, and the science of numbers is unchangeably available for all who can learn it, and is common to them all, so the rules of wisdom are true and unchangeable . . . Accordingly, you will never deny that there is an unchangeable truth which contains everything that is unchangeably true." Book II, paragraphs 29 and 33, found in *Augustine: Earlier Writings*, tr. by John H. S. Burleigh, Library of Christian Classics (Philadelphia: Westminster Press, 1953), Vol. VI, pp. 154, 156. Cf. also, "Of True Religion," paragraphs 53–57, *ibid.*, pp. 251–254. Also, *Concerning the Teacher*, Chapters XI and XII, *On the Immortality of the Soul*, Chapter I, IV, VI, XII, XV. The latter two works can be found in W. J. Oates, ed., *Basic Writings of St. Augustine* (New York: Random House, 1948), Vol. I.

16. For a brilliant example of a positive answer to this question, cf. Karl Rahner, *Spirit in the World*, esp. Part Two, Chapter III on "Abstraction." For a less impressive analysis of the dimension of ultimacy as it appears in noncognitive aspects of man's existence, cf. *Naming the Whirlwind*, Part II, Chapters 3 and 4.

17. Cf. esp. Polanyi's extended discussion of the "passions" that underlie and make possible scientific inquiry, *Personal Knowledge*, Chapter 6: "Intellectual Passions." Cf. also Lonergan, *op. cit.*, pp. 348–50.

18. Cf. Paul Tillich, "The Two Types of Philosophy of Religion," pp. 22–29, "Aspects of a Religious Analysis of Culture," pp. 40–43, and "Science and Theology," esp. pp. 130–131, in *Theology of Culture* (New York: Oxford University Press, 1959). For Heidegger's emphasis on the desire to know as basic to Dasein, and so a major form of "care," cf. *Being and Time*, tr. J. Macquarrie and E. Robinson (New York: Harper & Row, 1962), pp. 27, 38, and 78, and *An Introduction to Metaphysics*, tr. R. Manheim (Garden City, N.Y.: Doubleday Anchor, 1961), pp. 140–44.

19. For example, the following from Lonergan: "It is repugnant to me to place astrology and astronomy, alchemy and chemistry, legend and history, hypothesis and fact, on exactly the same footing. I am not content with theories, however brilliantly coherent, but insist on raising the further question, Are they true? What is that repugnance, that discontent, that insistence? They are just so many variations on the more basic expression that I am rationally conscious, that I demand sufficient reason, that I find it in the unconditioned, that I assent unreservedly to nothing less, that such demanding, finding, self-committing occur, not like the growth of my hair, but within a field of consciousness or awareness." Lonergan, *op. cit.*, pp. 323–24.

20. Polanyi, *op. cit.*, pp. 203, 216–22, 300; and *Science, Faith and Society*, pp. 43–45, 54–55.

21. A. N. Whitehead, *Process and Reality* (New York: The Macmillan Company, 1929), p. 67; cf. also *Adventures of Ideas*, pp. 180–81;

and *Science and the Modern World* (New York: The Macmillan Company, 1925), p. 197.

22. Toulmin, *Foresight and Understanding*, p. 57.

23. Polanyi, *Personal Knowledge*, esp. the section "The Premisses of Science," pp. 160–71; cf. also *Science, Faith and Society*, Chapter II.

24. Polanyi, *Personal Knowledge*, p. 166.

25. Cf. the following from Polanyi: "The inquiring scientist's intimations of a hidden reality are personal. They are his own beliefs, which—owing to his originality—as yet he alone holds. Yet they are not a subjective state of mind, but convictions held with universal intent, and heavy with arduous projects. It was he who decided what to believe, yet there is no arbitrariness in his decision. For he arrived at his conclusions by the utmost exercise of responsibility. He has reached responsible beliefs, born of necessity, and not changeable at will. In a heuristic commitment, affirmation, surrender, and legislation are fused into a single thought, bearing on a hidden reality" (*op. cit.*, p. 311). "Any act of factual knowing presupposes somebody who believes he knows what is being believed to be known. This person is taking a risk in asserting something, at least tacitly, about something believed to be real outside himself. . . . Every act of factual knowing has the structure of a commitment" (*ibid.*, p. 313). Cf. also Lonergan, *op. cit.*, p. 272.

26. As Lonergan puts this point: "The foundations of understanding yield concepts, definitions, objects of thought, suppositions, considerations. But man demands more. Every answer to a question for intelligence raises a further question for reflection. There is an ulterior motive to conceiving and defining, thinking and considering, forming suppositions, hypotheses, theories, systems. That motive appears when such activities are followed by the question, 'Is it so?' We conceive in order to judge" (*op. cit.*, p. 273). "If, above all, I want to understand, still I want to understand the facts. Inevitably, the achievement of understanding, however, stupendous, only gives rise to the further question, 'Is it so?' Inevitably, the progress of understanding is interrupted by the check of judgment" (*ibid*, p. 330). Cf. also p. 349.

27. This reference is found in Lonergan, *op. cit.*, p. 272. Polanyi makes the same point of the personal responsibility in judgments in *Science, Faith and Society*, p. 40.

28. Polanyi, *Personal Knowledge*, pp. 203–20, 302–3, 307–8, 315; cf. also Lonergan, *op. cit.*, p. 332.

29. That the notion of an infinity of internal relations, qualifying every proposition and thus making no invulnerable judgements possible, can finally subvert all real truth on the finite level is well illustrated in the thought of F. H. Bradley. For him, the world of interrelated "fact" must be appearance, and as such finite truths about it must forever remain relative error, because every "fact," every partial object of judgment, is so infinitely qualified by conditions about which we can never know that no certainty—on this side of the Absolute—is possible: "Take any object, and you find that, as it is, that object does not satisfy the mind. You cannot think it as real while you leave

it just as it comes. You are forced to go outside and beyond that first character, and to ask, What, Why and How. You must hence take your first object as included with something else in some wider reality. . . . On the other hand, you want to know the object itself and *not* something else. Therefore, while going beyond the object, you must not leave it but must still follow it. If you merely conjoin it with something outside that is different and not itself, this in principle is contradiction." F. H. Bradley, *Essays in Truth and Reality* (Oxford: The Clarendon Press, 1944), p. 227 n. For other examples of the same argument, cf. *Appearance and Reality* (Oxford: The Clarendon Press, 1946), pp. 25–26, 32, 46, 49, 58, 322, and 332.

To this gloomy logic that an infinity of relations constitutes a logical barrier to the possession of finite truth (or truth about the finite) and thus to *knowledge*, Lonergan would in such a situation make the following response: "But look, we *do* experience knowing; we *do* apprehend the fulfillment of the conditions. How we do so, we may not know; and that we know *all* is clearly impossible. Nevertheless, we do know, and we know that we know. That is, in fact we experience the conditions as *virtually* unconditioned, not as absolutely so; and this experience includes, or better, *is* the knowledge or awareness that we know. Bradley's problem was that he wished to find a rational foundation for the fundamental apprehensions that undergird rationality, and that is a 'category mistake.' The dual foundations of the possibility of knowing and of our certainty that we know, are (a) the undeniable statistical appearance in us all of acts of knowing, and (b) our self-affirmation of ourselves as knowers in and through this awareness of our rational consciousness that in this case we do in fact know."

30. The following give the skeleton of Lonergan's views of the process of judgment: "What we know is that to pronounce judgment without that reflective grasp is merely to guess; again, what we know is that, once that grasp has occurred, then to refuse to judge is just silly. Accordingly, the present section will be an effort to determine what precisely is meant by the sufficiency of the evidence for a prospective judgment" (*ibid.*, p. 279).

"To grasp the evidence as sufficient for a prospective judgment is to grasp the prospective judgment as virtually unconditioned. . . . The function of reflective understanding is to meet the question for reflection by transforming the prospective judgment from the status of a conditioned to the status of a virtually unconditioned; and reflective understanding effects this transformation by grasping the conditions of the conditioned and their fulfilment" (p. 280).

"Let us now distinguish between vulnerable and invulnerable insights. Insights are vulnerable when there are further questions to be asked on the same issue. . . . The conditioned is the prospective judgment, This or that direct or introspective insight is correct. The immanent law of cognitional process may be formulated from our analysis. Such an insight is correct, if there are no further, pertinent questions. . . . If, in fact, there are no further questions, then, in fact, the insight is invulnerable; if, in fact, the insight is invulnerable, then, in fact, the judgment approving it will be correct" (pp. 284–85). Cf. also *ibid.*, pp. 285–89, 319–22, 342–47.

31. Cf. Polanyi's interesting description of the necessity involved in a committed freedom: "Any devotion entails an act of self-compulsion. . . . *The freedom of the subjective person to do as he pleases is overruled by the freedom of the responsible person to act as he must.* . . . I shall go on, therefore, to repeat my fundamental belief that, in spite of the hazards involved, I am called upon to search for the truth and state my findings. . . . The paradox of self-set standards is eliminated; for in a competent mental act the agent does not do as he pleases, but compels himself forcibly to act as he believes he must." Polanyi, *op. cit.*, pp. 308, 309, 315. (Italics in the original.) Cf. also Lonergan, *op. cit.*, p. 279.

The reference in Augustine is from "On Free Will," paragraph 38: "To all who turn to it [truth] from the whole world, and love it, it is close at hand, everlasting, bound to no particular spot, never deficient. Externally it suggests, internally it teaches. All who behold it, it changes for the better, and by none is it changed for the worst. No one judges it, and no one without it judges aright. Hence it is evident beyond a doubt that wisdom is better than our minds, for by it alone they are made individually wise, and are made judges, not of it, but by it of all other things whatever." *Augustine: Earlier Writings,* p. 159. Cf. also "Of True Religion," paragraphs 53–57.

32. These remarks on the unconditioned character of my self-affirmation of myself as a knower in all my acts of cognition have, of course, a venerable tradition in philosophy, beginning with Augustine's comments on the impossibility of an ultimate skepticism. The particular form of these comments, however, like the analysis of judgment preceding them, is especially indebted to the thought of B. J. F. Lonergan. For example: "Still, if rational consciousness can criticize the achievement of science, it cannot criticize itself. The critical spirit can weigh all else in the balance, only on condition that it does not criticize itself. It is a self-assertive spontaneity that demands sufficient reason for all else but offers no justification for its demanding. It arises, fact-like, to generate knowledge of fact, to push the cognitional process from the conditioned structures of intelligence to unreserved affirmation of the unconditioned. It occurs. It will recur whenever the conditions for reflection are fulfilled. With statistical regularity those conditions keep being fulfilled. Nor is that all, for I am involved, engaged, committed. The disjunction between rationality and non-rationality is an abstract alternative but not a concrete choice. Rationality is my very dignity, and so closely to it do I cling, that I would want the best of reasons for abandoning it. . . . As I might not be, as I might be other than I am, so my knowing might not be and it might be other than it is. The ultimate basis of our knowing is not necessity but contingent fact, and the fact is established, not prior to our engagement in knowing, but simultaneously with it. The sceptic, then, is not involved in a conflict with absolute

necessity. He might not be; he might not be a knower. Contradiction arises when he utilizes cognitional process to deny it" (*op. cit.*, p. 332).

33. Augustine uttered this thought in many places. The following is a good example: "Everyone who knows that he has doubts knows with certainty something that is true, namely, that he doubts. He is certain, therefore, about *a* truth. Therefore everyone who doubts whether there be such a thing as *the* truth has at least *a* truth to set a limit to his doubt; and nothing can be true except truth be in it." "Of True Religion," paragraph 73, in *Earlier Writings*, pp. 262–63. Cf. also *The City of God*, Book XI, Chapter XXVI, in Oates, *op. cit.*, Vol. II, p. 168.

34. Cf. Lonergan: "Now the judgement of fact is not to the effect that something must be so or could not be otherwise; it merely states that something is so; hence the unconditioned that grounds it will be not formally but only virtually unconditioned" (*op. cit.*, p. 336). Cf. also pp. 319 and 322.

35. Paul Ricoeur, *Fallible Man*, tr. by Charles Kelbley (Chicago: Henry Regnery, 1965), pp. 7, 56–58, 67–68, 159–61.

36. Cf. Stephen Toulmin's discussion of "limiting questions" that transcend any given realm of discourse because they provide its presuppositions. Stephen Toulmin, *An Examination of the Place of Reason in Ethics* (New York: Cambridge University Press, 1964), Chapter XIV.

37. Plato, *Timaeus*, paragraph 28, p. 13, in *The Dialogues of Plato*, tr. by B. Jowett (New York: Random House, 1937), Vol. II; *Gorgias*, paragraph 523 (*op. cit.*, Vol. I, p. 583); *Phaedrus*, paragraph 265 (*ibid.*, p. 269); *Symposium*, paragraph 201 (*ibid.*, p. 327), and *Phaedo*, paragraph 107 f. (*ibid.*, p. 492 f.).

CHAPTER III.   The Uses of Myth in a Scientific Culture

1. Daniel Bell has given a good description of how a scientific culture approaches problems, and this *approach* is how he defines "technology": "Technology is not simply a 'machine,' but a systematic, disciplined approach to objectives, using a calculus of precision and measurement and a concept of system that are quite at variance with traditional and customary religious, aesthetic, and intuitive modes." Daniel Bell, "The Trajectory of an Idea," in *Daedalus: Toward the Year 2000*, p. 643.

2. Cf. Edmund R. Leach's frank admission that "the anthropologist's viewpoint is different [from that of the believer in myth]. He rejects the idea of a supernatural sender. He observes only a variety of possible receivers." "Genesis As Myth," in *Myth And Cosmos*, ed. by John Middleton (Garden City, N.Y.: The Natural History Press, 1967), p. 3. According to Leach, the anthropologist *ab initio* adopts a naturalist standpoint, excluding any "religious" understand we of myth. The scientific or philosophical grounds on which this reading of myth might be justified remain quite obscure, except possibly that a head count among the tribe of anthropologists would reveal this naturalism

to be their own most common "myth." That Professor Leach has also not escaped what he himself terms "the most striking of all religious phenomena—the passionate adherence to sectarian belief" (*ibid.*), is borne out by his own bitter remarks on another, "religious" approach to myth represented by the work of Mircea Eliade. Cf. Edmund Leach, "Sermons by a Man on a Ladder," *The New York Review of Books,* Vol. VII, No. 6 (October 20, 1966), pp. 28–31.

3. One of the most helpful definitions of myth, fully congruent with the themes of this book, is Paul Ricoeur's: "Myth will here be taken to mean what the history of religions now finds in it: not a false explanation by means of images and fables, but a traditional narration which relates to events that happened at the beginning of time and which has the purpose of providing grounds for the ritual actions of men of today and, in a general manner, establishing all the forms of action and thought by which a man understands himself in his world. . . . But in losing its explanatory pretensions the myth reveals its exploratory significance and its contribution to understanding, which we shall later call its symbolic function—that is to say, its power of discovering and revealing the bond between man and what he considers sacred. Paradoxical as it may seem, the myth, when it is thus demythologized through contact with scientific history and elevated to the dignity of a symbol, is a dimension of modern thought." Paul Ricoeur, *The Symbolism of Evil* (New York: Harper & Row, 1967), p. 5.

For an anthropologist's agreement that myth functions to give unity and legitimacy to the major activities of primitive society, cf. Robert Redfield: "The members of these societies 'believe in the sacred things; their sense of right and wrong springs from the unconscious roots of social feeling, and is therefore unreasoned, compulsive and strong.' People do the kinds of things they do, not because somebody just thought up that kind of thing, or because anybody ordered them to do so, but because it seems to the people to flow from the very necessity of existence that they do that kind of thing. The reasons given after the thing is done, in the form of myth and the dress of ceremony, assert the rightness of the choice." Robert Redfield, *The Primitive World* (Ithaca: Cornell University Press, 1965), p. 14.

The indebtedness of my discussion of traditional or ancient mythical discourse to my colleague, Mircea Eliade, is evident. The most important of his works in this connection are *Patterns of Comparative Religion,* tr. by R. Sheed (Cleveland: Meridian Books, 1966); *Cosmos and History,* tr. by W. R. Trask (New York: Harper Torchbooks, 1959); and *The Sacred And The Profane* (New York: Harper Torchbooks, 1961).

4. For the classical sources of this aspect of modernity, namely, that the only legitimate "explanation" of a process or event is to be found in the finite factors, natural or historical, that precede and surround it, cf. David Hume's essay on "Miracles" (Chapter X, *An Enquiry Concerning Human Understanding,* in *The Philosophical Works of David Hume,* Vol. IV [Edinburgh: A. Block and W. Tait, 1926]), and

Ernst Troeltsch's corresponding delineation of the structural limits of historical explanation in his work, *Der Historismus und seine Probleme* (Gesammelte Schriften, Vol. III [Tübingen: J. C. B. Mohr, 1922]). The same point is made in the philosophy of Whitehead in which the fundamental "principle of explanation," what he calls the ontological principle, states that "only actual entities provide legitimate reasons for things" and so alone may function as explanatory factors. Cf. *Process and Reality*, pp. 36–37.

5. As our first chapter outlined, much of the modern distrust of myth as a form of language was richly deserved, for past forms of mythical language (in our tradition enshrined in Biblical and theological assertions) claimed to inform us of matters of fact on religious authority—and were almost always proved wrong by the development of science. After their long experience of seeing religious truths thus "disproved" by science, many modern men have reasonably concluded that myth as such was merely a form of prescientific information about the world, and therefore superstitious. That modern men do not and frequently cannot see the *other* function and meaning of mythical language poses one of the deepest problems for theology and for cultural health today.

6. In his remarkable book on the Enlightenment, an epoch which represented the first full expression of this "modern" attitude toward man's widest environment, Peter Gay characterizes that age as "a rebirth of paganism," and he means primarily by that that it possessed a *critical* spirit, critical of all merely believed myths and unexamined authorities, a spirit whose most important result was that henceforth man lived in a "disenchanted" (or desacralized) world: "To be disenchanted is not to give way to jaded, supercilious scepticism, but to shift canons of proof and direction of worship. What is at work in the incredulity of the philosophes is not the shrinking of experience to the hard, the measurable, the prosaic, the surface of events; it is, on the contrary, an expansion of the natural. The disenchanted universe of the Enlightenment is a natural universe. . . . *All things are equally subject to criticism*; to say this was to move confidently in a world free—or rather, waiting to be freed—from enchantment."

And he concludes the volume with this summarizing characterization of David Hume, and through him of the Enlightenment as a whole: "Hume, therefore, more decisively than many of his brethren in the Enlightenment, stands at the threshold of modernity and exhibits its risks and its possibilities. Without melodrama but with the sober eloquence one would expect from an accomplished classicist, Hume makes plain that since God is silent, man is his own master; he must live in a disenchanted world, submit everything to criticism, and make his own way." Peter Gay, *The Enlightenment: An Interpretation* (New York: Alfred A. Knopf, 1967), pp. 148–50 and 419 respectively. (Italics in the original.)

7. Cf. esp. the thought of Ludwig Feuerbach, *The Essence of Christianity*, and *Lectures on The Essence of Religion*, for the earliest

expression of this understanding of the mythical language of religion. In modern times possibly the best and most appreciative expressions of this anthropocentric interpretation of myth has been that of George Santayana in *Reason in Religion* (New York: Charles Scribner's Sons, 1936), *The Realm of Essence* (New York: Charles Scribner's Sons, 1927), and *Platonism and the Spiritual Life* (New York: Charles Scribner's Sons, 1927), and John Dewey in *A Common Faith* (New Haven: Yale University Press, 1934).

8. For a more detailed description of this historical development, cf. *Naming the Whirlwind*, Part I, Chapter 2.

9. It is this point that Karl Löwith makes central to the development of the "contemporary spirit," namely, that this spirit begins when man ceases to understand himself in terms of an "essence" given him in the total cosmic order, and understands himself in terms of his freedom to create and enact his own being in existence. For Löwith, therefore, existentialist thought, in denying an essence of man prior to his "existence," and thus in asserting *only* his existence in freedom, is the characteristic expression of the modern attitude. Cf. Karl Löwith, *Nature, History and Existentialism* (Evanston: Northwestern University Press, 1966), esp. Chapters I, II, and III.

The Biblical background of the historical consciousness of modern man—that he exists in history, that history is "open," an arena for his creativity and decision, and thus that he faces *forward* into the *new* rather than backward into the "already established"—has long been a theme for students of Scripture. Neo-orthodoxy in this connection stressed the Biblical roots of the modern sense (a) of linear and purposive time instead of cyclical and nondirected time, and (b) of the uniqueness of each moment and so of historical decisions, generally finding these roots, as did Augustine before them, in the crucial events of divine revelation which gave to "a moment" an eternal significance (cf. Augustine, *The City of God*, Book XI, Chapters IV and VI, pp. 146–48, and esp. Book XII, Chapter XIII, p. 192, in Oates, *op. cit.*). Contemporary eschatological theology, on the other hand, tends to locate these roots, not in the Biblical experience of ultimately significant *past* events, but in the expectation of a future "new" which resulted from the *eschatological* consciousness of Biblical faith. Cf. Jürgen Moltmann, *The Theology of Hope*, Chapter II, esp. pp. 106–12.

10. This concept, inspired of course by Nietzsche, has become the main thrust of the radical theology of Thomas J. J. Altizer: the "religious" search for origins and the worship of the transcendent are, he says, causes of repression; the transcendent God must die if man is to be free, and with the loss of this crushing heteronomy, man's resentment, envy, and hostility will also vanish. Cf. *The Gospel of Christian Atheism* (Philadelphia: Westminster Press, 1966). For some of the same Nietzschean themes, cf. Richard Rubenstein's *After Auschwitz* (Indianapolis: Bobbs-Merrill, 1966).

11. There is a long tradition that has taken conscience as the central and even initiating point of relationship between man and God. This

is surely true of both Luther and Calvin; it becomes even more prominent in Kant, Ritschl, W. R. Sorley, John Baillie, Emil Brunner, and, in our own day, Gerhard Ebeling. For the latter, cf. *Word and Faith* (Philadelphia: Fortress Press, 1963), esp. pp. 349, 356, and 360.

12. One exception to this has been Robert Ardrey's interesting feeling that if modern political man knew that his first progenitor had been a predatory killer, this knowledge might shatter all our hopes for world peace today. Apparently Ardrey, though quite modern in his anthropological theory, shares the ancient mythical feeling that the original form of man, did we but know that form, might exert a potent "exemplar" force on contemporary life. Cf. Robert Ardrey, *African Genesis* (New York: Atheneum Press, 1961).

13. Examples of this *temporalistically* dominated theology, in which little interest in or notion of "eternity" appears, abound both in this country and on the Continent. The most obvious are, of course, the "process" theologies, stemming from the tradition of Whitehead, namely, the thought of Charles Hartshorne, Daniel D. Williams, John B. Cobb, Jr., and Schubert M. Ogden. Another group has, in all probability, Hegelian roots, best exemplified in this century by Paul Tillich for whom God (alias Being-Itself) is a dynamic reality whose aseity is based, not on His separation from time and change, but on His creative power to overcome the threat of non-Being. Most surprising as forms of "modernism" are the Biblical theologies of the recent period: (1) the neo-orthodox movement itself where God has generally been characterized by "freedom" rather than by aseity, and by His dynamic activity in history rather than by His changeless rest above history, and (2) the contemporary "eschatological theology" in which He is the God "who comes" in the *future* rather than the God who transcends in eternity all the phases of time. Oscar Cullmann's *Christ and Time* (tr. by F. V. Filson [Philadelphia: Westminster Press, 1964]) and Jürgen Moltmann's *Theology of Hope* are, perhaps, the clearest examples of the temporalistic character of both of these types of modern Biblical theology. The universality of this basic temporalistic structure in recent theology, *whatever* the theological method pursued, leads one to surmise that a temporalistic concept of reality and so of deity is probably more a presupposition of the modern consciousness as such than the result *either* (a) of a particular form of modern metaphysics, say the process sort, *or* (b) of a sharper Scriptural exegesis and so a profounder understanding of the Bible than other less temporalistic ages were able to muster.

14. The sense that the "given" is merely material for man's creative remaking, that freedom is discovered or realized through giving new forms to traditional materials rather than through reenacting the traditional, is expressed, of course, most potently in existentialist literature, especially that of Sartre and Heidegger. However, there can be little doubt that the same interpretation of the relation of the traditional "given" to freedom is present in the thought of John Dewey, for whom the central function of critical intelligence is that of testing and refashioning all traditional and given forms, social institutions,

standards and beliefs. It also appears in the thought of A. N. Whitehead, for whom the main function of freedom is to effect the ingression
of novel and creative possibilities into precedent actuality. Novelty is
here almost a self-sufficient value, good in its own right regardless of
content—almost the opposite of the ancient consciousness in which
what "has always been" has sacred character, and for that reason
alone.

15. In this discussion of the "myth" of Evolution, we do not refer
to the biological theory of that name which, of course, is a vastly
respected theory in a particular science and so explanatory of a
limited range of questions. We refer, rather, to the expansion of that
concept into a law of universal process by means of which every sort
of major natural or historical change is to be interpreted. Such a
universal notion is not testable as are the hypotheses of a special
science, and the concept itself clearly functions as a myth in our wider
cultural life. Cf. Stephen Toulmin's description of the "myth" of
evolution, in "Contemporary Scientific Mythology," *op. cit.*, pp. 47–66.

16. The movement from a cosmic mythology to an anthropocentric
one is, in the lingo of evolutionary science, perhaps best visible in the
tendency of contemporary evolutionists to distinguish, first, biological
evolution from "cultural evolution," and to distinguish, secondly, the
cultural and historical developments of the *past*, which were determined by uncomprehended genetic, social, and technical factors, from
present and future possibilities of *deliberate* control over these factors
through modern science. Thus in an age of science man, so to speak,
"takes over" the direction of his own evolutionary destiny from both
cosmic and past cultural-historical processes.

The reason we consider the category "cultural evolution" confused
is that it combines concepts which tend to exclude one another, and
thus it forms a starkly paradoxical synthesis. "Evolution" implies a
nonintentional and so determined process of change which is neither
intended nor stoppable, something that happens whether we humans
will it or not. Thus, happily for those who like to use it in this
context, the term "evolution" unites the sense of scientific rigor (it
sounds like a natural law) with the comforting implication that as
a creative process far transcending us, we can depend on it. "Culture"
has a quite different feel: it contains intentional elements, we can
therefore control it in part, and, above all, culture is subject to the
weird twists and arbitrary turns of the category of *history*. What the
term "cultural evolution" is seeking to talk about is, therefore, the
immensely complex reality of social or historical change, a reality
compounded *both* of determining forces *and* of intentional and so
*non*determinable forces. It seeks to comprehend this complexity by
using a simplistic model taken from the nonintentional realms of
cosmic processes and biology, and then to make it adequate to this
new complexity that history introduces into the mixture by adding
quite arbitrarily the utterly different category of "culture." What is,
then, in actuality a fairly mysterious complexity, namely history, is
transposed in this phrase into a stark contradiction in which mutually

exclusive terms are arbitrarily jammed together, the one side implying determinism and the other intentionality and choice, with no mediation between these two offered for our thought. Is the process of "cultural evolution" *determined* by forces that can be scientifically understood, or is it *controllable* so that we can intentionally manipulate it—for it cannot simply be both! Are we in turn dependent upon its unfolding, or must its direction depend upon ourselves? The phrase implies both sides at once of these questions, and so in fact it implies nothing. Especially does this paradox become a contradiction when the modern anthropologist states that since we can now understand its *determining* forces, we can now *control* cultural evolution; and that further, as a consequence, we are now solely responsible for its future direction through our "choices" and "decisions"! Incidentally, he thereby affirms as well a quite naïve faith in the possibility of human control over human and historical destiny.

"Cultural evolution" is thus a way of talking about the ambiguities and terrors of history that makes anthropologists feel at home. It makes them feel at home both with regard to a method that is familiar to them and with regard to their own existential situation as human beings worried about the future. But the term has connotations in two directions which distort its object: as "evolution" it is too deterministic a word for history; as "controllable") because we can understand the principles of its determination) it emphasizes freedom too much to comprehend the ambiguity of man's history. Thus as a concept it does little but comfort the anthropologists with regard to their ability to understand and to control the development of history and the frightening ambiguities of the future.

For further examples of this shift to *man's* present capacity to control evolution, see the following note, number 17. Meanwhile, for the more basic distinction between "biological" and "cultural" evolution, cf. the article "Cultural Evolution Today," by the anthropologist Julian H. Steward, in *Changing Man: The Threat and the Promise*, ed. by K. Haselden and P. Hefner (Garden City, N.Y.: Doubleday, 1967), pp. 49–62:

"*Is evolution now chiefly cultural?* Since no important biological change in *Homo sapiens* has occurred during the past 40,000 years, the tremendous evolutionary [*sic!*] changes in culture within this period must have nonbiological explanations. . . . During the past few hundred years—less than one-fifth of one per cent of the time modern man has occupied the earth—the industrial revolution has transformed Euro-American culture and disseminated its influence throughout the world [note that the agent in this process is a "force" and not *man*]. But this incredible acceleration of cultural evolution and the emergence of many distinctive cultural traditions have had no effect on biological evolution" (*ibid.*, p. 52; italics in the original). "The nature of cultural evolution is best exemplified in the substantive terms of particular factors and processes that have recently been postulated with some certainty. But, because the method is now empirical, it is not yet possible to offer universal principles or explanations" (p. 55). "But [now] change seems to be getting out of hand. Every individual and every nation confronts conflicting choices and expectations, and there are no clear guidelines for behavior. To achieve some kind of stabilization and sense of direction, deeper understanding of the nature of change is needed . . ." (pp. 61–62).

Let us note three factors in these remarks: (1) Cultural evolution is understood as being a *process* with certain determining factors which we are about to understand, if not fully, at least with real clarity—as in other sciences. Thus it is a heuristic notion patterned on the model of biological or cosmic evolution, or more directly on the model with which the anthropologist seeks to understand prehistorical societies. (2) This notion covers the general fields *both* of human prehistory *and* of history, that is, it brings the human story right up to the present. In effect, therefore, it *replaces* the category of history, and thus in claiming to understand the process of "cultural evolution," the anthropologist is in fact modestly claiming finally to uncover the principles effecting the course of history as a whole, that is, to propound a philosophy of history! (Who said anthropology was the most aggressively imperialist of modern sciences?) (3) Finally, let us note that despite the deterministic implications in points (1) and (2), implications which make these two points intelligible, the *present* is viewed as dominated by man's freedom, responsibility, and knowledge—though where that "freedom" has been hiding in the past of the human story is left unexamined. Has freedom really arisen *only* with science and its understanding of "cultural evolution"? Thus quite unknowingly, many modern scientists share with Hegel the comfortable feeling that the human Spirit has in themselves at last reached self-consciousness and so self-direction.

17. For the most potent formulations of this "anthropocentric" view of future evolution, besides the volume by Julian Huxley referred to above, cf. the writings of Theodosius Dobzhansky and George Gaylord Simpson, the two most distinguished contemporary evolutionists. In the view of each, evolutionary process, which heretofore has been (for science) a blind, random, purposeless biological process, has spawned a purposive, free creature who can know and be self-aware, and thus can, now that he *knows*, direct his evolutionary destiny. The future course of evolution, therefore, does not at all depend on a cosmic determinism but on the results of human choices, on a mature and responsible use of human freedom and knowledge. Since science has given to us the freedom to control evolution, it is now up to us: "Man has risen, not fallen. He can choose to develop his capacities as the highest animal and to try to rise still farther, or he can choose otherwise. The choice is his responsibility, and his alone. There is no automatism that will carry him upward without choice or effort, and there is no trend solely in the right direction. [Where did the *determining factors* we are about to uncover in "cultural evolution" disappear to?] Evolution has no purpose; man must supply this for himself. . . . The best human ethical standard must be relative to man and is to be sought rather in the new evolution, peculiar to man,

than in the old, universal to all organisms. The old evolution was and is essentially amoral. The new evolution involves knowledge, including the knowledge of good and evil. The most essential material factor in the new evolution seems to be this: knowledge, together, necessarily, with its spread and inheritance." George Gaylord Simpson, *The Meaning of Evolution* (New York: Mentor Books, 1957), pp. 155–56; cf. also, pp. 174, 179–81.

"Man has not only evolved, he is evolving. This is a source of hope in the abyss of despair. In a way Darwin has healed the wound inflicted by Copernicus and Galileo. Man is not the center of the universe physically, but he may be the spiritual center. Man and man alone knows that the world evolves and that he evolves with it. By changing what he knows about the world man changes the world that he knows: and by changing the world in which he lives man changes himself. Changes may be deteriorations or improvement; the hope lies in the possibility that changes resulting from knowledge may also be directed by knowledge. Evolution need no longer be a destiny imposed from without; it may conceivably be controlled by man, in accordance with his wisdom and his values." T. Dobzhansky, *Mankind Evolving* (New Haven: Yale University Press, 1962), pp. 346–47. Cf. also, *ibid.*, p. 22; T. Dobzhansky, *Evolution, Genetics and Man* (New York: John Wiley & Sons, 1965), pp. 334, 377–78; and "Evolution: Implications for Religion," in Haselden and Hefner, *op. cit.*, pp. 144, 152–55.

In summing up this viewpoint of the scientific community about evolution and our destiny, Victor Ferkiss, first quoting Dr. John Heller, writes as follows: " 'The logical climax of evolution can be said to have occurred when, as is now imminent, a sentient species deliberately [*sic*] and directly assumes control of its own evolution,' is the way a leading medical researcher describes man's new status in the cosmos. . . . Together these changes constitute an existential revolution that poses a new challenge for mankind. If man can do or be whatever he wishes, how shall he choose? What should be his criteria of choice? In the past, nature and ignorance set limits to man's freedom and his follies, now they need no longer stand in his way, and technological man will be free even to destroy the possibility of freedom itself." Victor Ferkiss, *op. cit.*, p. 111.

When the modern reader compares these statements about man's origins with those quoted from classical theology in the first chapter (fn. 3), he is struck by the factual inaccuracy of the latter—clearly the theologians had the actual story all wrong. However, deeper reflection indicates that these modern modes of understanding man as now capable of controlling his destiny are on another level perhaps even more in error, and reflect little wisdom with regard to the manner in which man actually exists and actualizes his freedom in history. The question, therefore, as to which one *understands* humanity better, is by no means settled by the test of factual accuracy.

18. Cf. the image of man as autonomous, self-aware and so loving in the writings of Erich Fromm, esp. *Man for Himself* (London:

Routledge & Kegan Paul, 1949), and the image of the new unrepressed, bodily, polymorphous man in Norman O. Brown's *Life Against Death* (New York: Vintage Books, 1959).

19. Cf. the following extravagant statement of man's new "freedom" from Ferkiss: "But what could take place in the realm of cultures so fundamental as to alter the basic nature of the human animal? . . . Simply by giving man almost infinite power to change his world and to change himself. In the words of Emmanuel Mesthene . . . 'We have now, or know how to acquire, the technical capability to do very nearly anything we want. Can we transplant human hearts, control personality, order the weather that suits us, travel to Mars or Venus? Of course we can, if not now or in five or ten years, then certainly in 25 or in 50 or 100.' . . . For these new powers are not merely extensions of the old. The whole is greater than the sum of its parts, and absolute power over himself and his environment puts man in a radically new moral position." Ferkiss, *op. cit.*, pp. 20–21. However, on page 23, Ferkiss realistically pens the following sentence: "The missiles are in their silos as you read this."

The biophysicist Leroy Augenstein puts this increment of freedom in its proper theological language when he says, "Instead of downgrading man, science is literally forcing man to play God." In Haselten and Hefner, *op. cit.*, p. 98.

20. This is a perfect likeness to the image we have sought here to describe: the sense of the unilmited potentiality of human freedom to use scientific knowledge creatively to control our destiny, the noticeable shift from cosmic, evolutionary symbols to anthropocentric autonomous symbols, and the direct relation of scientific inquiry to man's control over his fate. These are the elements of the image, or "myth," which, we believe, is the foundation for most of the confidence and the hopes of the intellectual élite of our culture.

It is amusing and even ironic to note that many social scientists, who echo Seaborg's hopes, correctly scoffed at Barry Goldwater's emphasis on the control *economic* man has over his own personal destiny. Said Goldwater, those who can and will to, make it; those who do not work hard enough, end up on the welfare rolls. On the contrary, retorted the savants, social science reveals that the economic possibilities and opportunities which certain classes enjoy are *not* created merely by their own capabilities and wills, but rather have been rigidly determined by their given or "fated" social position, and thus that the conservative "myth" of the control by individual freedom and hard work over economic destiny is really a rationalization for the freedom of the élite to gain and to retain their given economic privileges. And yet the same social scientists believe firmly that the social scientist, if not the business executive, can control many of these same fates and so eradicate the power of the "historical given" in historical life. The conservative myth seems to believe in the sacral autonomy of pragmatic, energetic, hardheaded executive man; the liberal, academic myth believes in the powerful gnosis of scientific man. Each alternative assumes in its own way that the man who "understands" and "wills" can control significant destiny by manipulating the pervasive structures of society for his own purposes.

For other assertions of man's new freedom over all relevant fates, let us recall the quotations from Dobzhansky, Simpson, and Ferkiss above in ns. 17 and 19.

21. As another example of the inevitable use of the intentional language of "freedom" in authors writing *about* science and its uses, cf. (besides ns. 16, 17, 19, and 20 above) this from Ferkiss: "Our concern here is twofold. First, we wish to discover the role played by science and technology in the shaping of all aspects of the new era—social and cultural as well as economic. Second, we wish to isolate those technological elements underlying industrialism that combined have raised the position of technology and civilization to a 'critical mass.' It is this 'critical mass' that presently threatens to explode the civilization created by industrialism so that humanity is left with the choice of creating a new civilization or else living— or perhaps dying—in chaos." Ferkiss, *op. cit.*, p. 35. Let us note: (1) how the past and present, which science can understand, is even here described as determined by impersonal forces; but (2) the future is starkly (quite unrealistically, we would say) characterized by absolute choices. One wonders how, if the past (when *it* was "future") was thus constituted by absolute choices, it can now as past be described and so understood in such deterministic terms—or has this freedom just *now* begun with science, and so is it characteristic only of *our* future? Surely here is the *real* myth Ferkiss is talking about in his book!

22. The paradox is complete when the behaviorist B. F. Skinner is described in terms that almost ecstatically (ironically?) use in one sentence the language both of determinism and of freedom to describe (a) our knowledge of this determination and (b) our free use of this knowledge: "But what is more interesting about Skinner is the implication of his central thesis, which cannot be denied: it is now theoretically possible, given a certain investment of resources and access to the persons involved, to control human personal and social development is a systematic way. Whether one has regarded previous situations as freedom or bondage to blind faith, as preferable or not, is beside the point. The point is that now a choice can and must be made" (*ibid.*, p. 89).

23. The cultural evolutionist, Julian H. Steward, makes this implication of the scientific method *vis-à-vis* man quite explicit: "I emphasize casuality because any assumption that teleological or orthogenetic principles, divine intervention or free will are at work would nullify scientific explanation. To those who disagree [cf. Dobzhansky and Simpson, *et al*!] I can only say that science must proceed *as if* natural laws operate consistently and without exceptions, as if all cultures and all aspects of human behavior had determinants —no matter how difficult the task of unraveling the intricately interrelated phenomenon." Steward, *op. cit.*, in Haselden and Hefner, *op. cit.*, pp. 50–51. (Italics in the original.) How this deterministic

presupposition of a scientific understanding of man fits in with his own challenge to us to exercise responsible choice through our new knowledge (is this free will?) in the future (pp. 61–62) is left unanswered. Apparently the contradiction (and it is little else) is resolved *temporalistically*: man in the past and present has been utterly determined; in the future he is or can be utterly or largely free—and the difference is, not unsurprisingly, the appearance of science.

Another, more sophisticated expression of the same paradox is the following from Ernst Nagel, stating the principles which he regards to be of the essence of naturalism. The first principle of naturalism, says Nagel, is "the existential and causal primacy of organized matter in the executive order of nature." On the other hand, human reason, continues Nagel when speaking of our human hopes, while "not an omnipotent instrument for the achievement of human goods," is still "the only instrument we do possess, and it is not a contemptible one," that is, it is a potent instrument against those evils that can be remedied. Ernst Nagel, *Logic without Metaphysics* (Glencoe: Free Press, 1956), pp. 7 and 18.

24. For this writer one of the most brilliant resolutions of this problem is that of A. N. Whitehead. For Whitehead the concrete actuality of an entity is its self-formation, and thus the language of freedom and intentionality is appropriate to the *internal* constitution of all occasions, including of course men, and accordingly this language characterizes the way we speak of a *contemporary* occasion in relation to its own future. On the other hand, occasions that *have occurred* are experienced and so are understood from the *outside*, as objective events with only external relations and thus without freedom or intentionality. Because, therefore, science views things as objectified and so as totally determined, it presents to us only an "abstractive" or "partial" aspect of the whole of concreteness and is thus not to be taken as exhaustive with regard to our understanding either of nature or of man. Another, ultimately less satisfactory way of resolving this issue is the extentialist-personalist mode of distinguishing two utterly disparate ways of knowing: scientific knowledge of "its" and existential knowledge of "thous" or persons. As we are seeking to argue, however, books on science inevitably avail themselves of *both* of these two modes of knowing, and thus unescapably call for the kind of systematic view so ably represented by Whitehead.

25. Certainly the most creative attempts in recent theology to deal with these "paradoxes" of man's nature in terms of Christian symbols have been Reinhold Niebuhr's *The Nature and Destiny of Man* (New York: Charles Scribner's Sons, 1941–43), Vol. I, and Paul Tillich's *Systematic Theology* (Chicago: University of Chicago Press, 1951–63), Vols. I–III. For the most stimulating and powerful treatment in recent philosophy of the paradox of the voluntary and the involuntary, its relation to fallibility and to actual evil, see the monumental volumes of Paul Ricoeur: *Freedom and Nature: The Voluntary and the Involuntary*, tr. by E. V. Kohak (Evanston: Northwestern University Press, 1966); *Fallible Man*; and *The Symbolism of Evil*;

and also M. Merleau-Ponty, *Phenomenology of Perception*, tr. by Colin Smith (London: Routledge & Kegan Paul, 1962), esp. Parts I and III.

26. In fact, Victor Ferkiss defines, "technological man," the new species he devoutly hopes for, in terms of the application of this model (of the engineer) to his social and personal problems: "Let us assume that technological man, were he to exist, would apply to his own life the same standards of rationality that are associated with science and technology: the making of conscious choices based on knowledge of reality and its interrelations, the appreciation of the extent to which choice is conditioned by the inexorable facts of nature and of how freedom must be maximized within the limitations prescribed by those facts and an appreciation of the relationship between ends and means, parts and the whole" (*op. cit.*, p. 195)—and this, he adds later, is the condition necessary if "humanity is to retain [*sic*] control of its destiny" (p. 205); and "The race's only salvation is in the creation of technological man" (p. 245).

27. On many points a wise realist, Ferkiss fairly leaves the earth when he ponders the image of technological man as opposed to present-day "economic" and "political" man, who are the source and perpetuators of our evil. (Here one may say is *real* mythical thinking—not that technological man is unhappily still myth and not reality, as Ferkiss bemoans, but that his *idea* of technological man, like the labels "economic" and "political man," illustrates a mythical way of speaking of man.) Thus the problem of the "control of the controllers" does not, for Ferkiss, involve the control of an elite of technological man; rather it involves giving *technological* man rather than *political* man control over social change: "The problem is to put technological man in power rather than the men of a previous breed [*sic*] who do not have any sense of how these scientific resources might best be used" (*ibid.*, p. 265).

28. The "extra scientific" character of the problems raised by the *uses* of science is very forcibly put by sociologist Karl H. Hertz: "When we consider social policy, we must recognize that scientists may in their prescription of what is 'good' for man be expressing the prejudices of their upbringing or their commitment to a Platonic political ideology in which they are the philosopher-kings who can shape the future. In raising questions about the competence of biologists to determine the optimal genotype, I am not impugning their scientific knowledge; I am pointing out that when one moves from knowledge to practice, one inevitably becomes entangled in questions that are not really scientific. That is, to prescribe the genetic constitution of the man of the future, to bring him into being via sperm banks and genetic surgery, is to claim to know what the ideal human being ought to be. This is not biology but ethics and moral philosophy." Karl H. Hertz, "What Man Can Make of Man," in Haselden and Hefner, *op. cit.*, p. 104. Compare this realistic view of technological man with that of Ferkiss in the foregoing footnote!

29. The reason that Ferkiss can miss this fairly obvious truth about will-power, even or especially technological man's will-power, is

that his thought about man is veritably mythical in the worst sense, that is, caught in abstractions that befuddle rather than clarify understanding. Confident that "technological man" is, as we noted, not only rational but virtuous, he asks why, granted the great advances in technology that we have already made, has this paragon not yet appeared? (*op. cit.*, pp. 117, 153, etc.). The answer is, he says, that economic man and political man (whoever *they* may be) have not yet developed out of the animal greeds and selfishnesses of early bourgeois industrial life, and so "prevent" technical man from appearing on the scene (pp. 153, 195, 307): "The political and governmental structures, even in the most technological advanced nations, render man bewildered and impotent, a prisoner of his most primitive atavisms and the plaything of the fates" (p. 196). (Since, apparently, on this view man is the completely determined victim of objective social structures and forces, it is hard to see how the godlike technological man could ever develop at all!)

Granted this inexplicable but gloomy fact (that economic and political man have not kept moral pace with their more virtuous technological brother) Ferkiss begins to sound not the note of utter optimism heard before, but one of despair: "For what emerges as the pattern of the future is not technological man so much as neoprimitive man trapped in a technological environment" (p. 207). Urging us to be "willing to exercise self-control," he concludes that "if human nature is unchangeable then social systems are likewise unreformable," and "if this sounds utopian, one can only agree with the biologist John Rader Platt, who has observed that utopia may be the only viable social system in the world to come" (p. 262).

We have dealt with this book at length because it represents, we feel, a particularly clear case of "mythical thought," even when it feels it is most scientific: that is, abstract and nonempirical images of man that are used to understand man's basic nature and destiny, and thus to resolve our most fundamental problems of historical understanding and so our deepest anxieties about the future. That the images of technological, political, and economic man are in fact monstrous abstractions goes without saying; that they tend to obscure the complexities of history is also evident; and finally that they pose a choice between exaggerated optimism or exaggerated despair, these last quotations amply show. In this sense they are perfect cases of what we have discussed in the text, namely, anthropocentric mythical images used to understand the deepest problems of our human social and historical existence.

30. Although caught as we noted in his own myths, Ferkiss is intensely realistic about the irrational and unplanned, and so uncontrolled, character of *current* and so *actual* technological advance: ". . . everything that science can discover and technology create will be looked for or not, introduced or not, widely exploited or not, without reference to any standard other than private interest save when eccentric individuals or groups seek to impose their own personal convictions about the common good. But no means exist for the na-

tional community or the race as a whole to decide what shall be done" (*ibid.*, p. 191). That last telling sentence *should* reveal how "mythical" was the picture of Mankind "deciding" its fate in the near future, and thus somewhat reduce the sense of our potential control over destiny—but apparently such myths, functioning as the basis for confidence in an awesome future, defy the empirical evidence among members of the scientific community as readily as they do in the churches!

31. This phrase is taken from a remarkable, stirring, and disturbing address (as yet unpublished) by Norman V. Peterson, senior systems analyst for Gruen Associates, Inc., Los Angeles, at the University of Redlands in January, 1969. Peterson said, among other things: "To a great extent I see our technological order as both a tyranny and a frolic! Much of our technological order is directed to affluent wants, to violence, or to destructive products. . . . Escalation of all dimensions of technology proceeds without letup, without serious inquiry of the destructive side effects or implications of innovation, without a search for alternative solutions, or alternative allocations of resources over time. 'Supersonic' technology is the new mechanism for fueling a whirlwind economy based more on affluent wants and destructive productions than on structural needs . . ." (mimeographed copy, pp. 3 and 5).

"If one were to canvass the technical fraternity and its management community it would be overwhelmingly concluded that the interesting problems were those of supersonic transports, bombers and fighters, hypersonic guided missiles, lunar vehicles, CBR's, the world of the computer, and the next new technical novelty. But a close tour through our urban complex would soon reveal that the vital problems were at the interface between technology and man. It would be discernible that today much of our industrial, governmental and academic complex is involved in a technological frolic—the pursuit of unnecessary problems using unnecessary technology" (*op. cit.*, pp. 16–17).

Such an indictment of the irrational but ever-accelerating course of technological developments from one who knows cannot but render uneasy those others of us who do not know!

32. Ferkiss recognizes that at present the development of technology is neither rationally guided nor creatively motivated—though this is the fault of economic and political man: "As we have already seen, virtually every possible extension of man's powers over nature and himself almost certainly will be made or not made, shaped in one direction or another, not by considerations of what is good for man but what is good for some men; problems that are basically scientific and ethical will be decided in economic terms" (*op. cit.*, p. 149). Granting his clear recognition of this evidence, it is surely strange that Ferkiss should (a) scoff at those writers who fear technology and its influence on future society, and (b) regard the development of technology as virtually a principle of salvation for future society. Obviously he feels that some fundamental change in the human social,

and so historical, situation will occur when the new rational rather than the old selfish man will be born, and then this *use* of technology for selfish economic or political ends will no longer be the case—which is eschatology indeed!

33. The two great Platonic "visions" of an ordered society every element of whose life reflected rational planning, are, of course, *The Republic* and *The Laws*.

CHAPTER IV. **Epilogue: Myth, Philosophy, and Theology**

1. It is clear that the "anthropomorphic" character of much theological language in our tradition is closely associated with the character of myth as a form of language about God, for myth is, as Bultmann stated, to speak of God in some of the same ways one speaks of man. Generally, however, most of us conceive of "anthropomorphism" as giving to God the physical characteristics of man, a white beard, a strong right arm, everlasting arms, etc.; we should realize that anthropomorphism, and with it mythical language, is not confined to such literalism, but includes as well all analogical language about divine intentions, purposes, plans, promises, speech, emotions, faithfulness, and "activity"—all of which are words whose ordinary usage arises in talking about men and women, and thus *prima facie* they imply a circumscribed, intentional, personal being, existing within the phenomenal order of space and time. As we shall argue, this mode of language about God has not only raised many of the problems concerning matters of fact which we have already discussed, but also has helped to assure that relationship to *history* and to concrete *fact* characteristic of the Judaeo-Christian tradition, and to express that conviction of the personal, "inward" nature of God so central to Jewish and Christian piety.

2. Cf. Paul Ricoeur's comment that myth is the first "hermeneutic" of primary religious symbols, giving to them a consistent thematic interpretation in the form of a story, and thus leading on inevitably to the third level of speculation or gnosis. Paul Ricoeur, *The Symbolism of Evil*, p. 237.

3. For two excellent treatments of this subject, cf. Henri Frankfort *et al.*, *The Intellectual Adventure of Ancient Man* (Chicago: University of Chicago Press, 1946), esp. the Introduction and the Conclusion; and Werner Jaeger, *The Theology of the Early Greek Philosophers* (Oxford: The Clarendon Press, 1947).

Heidegger has, as usual, some very interesting things to say about this development within Western culture from myth to thought. Asking "What call directed this thinking to begin?" (p. 167), he argues that the essence of early Greek thought is to be found in the *response* of these men to the call of Being, a responding to this call in the form of thought—and that thus the "destiny" of Western thought was there established that it be thought *provoked* by its object, by what is most important to be thought about, rather than a merely autonomous development of "advancing cultural sophistication," which is the usual interpretation. For most historians of culture (as many quotations in our last chapter indicated) "man makes himself" and nowhere more clearly than when he ceased to be enmeshed in a mythic consciousness and succeeded in raising himself to the level of reflective thought—and now, beyond that, to the level of science. Heidegger disagrees: man is provoked into thought by the mystery and power of its object; his destiny is fulfilled when that object remains in full view, and is lost or darkened when—in the name of what he thinks it is important to think about—man "forgets" Being and concentrates only on the beings and their interrelations. Martin Heidegger, *What Is Called Thinking?* tr. by F. D. Wieck and J. G. Gray (New York: Harper & Row, 1968), Part II, Lectures V and VI.

4. Cf. Harnack's well-known thesis that the philosophical components of Patristic thought resulted primarily from (a) the movement of the simple, nontheological gospel out of its Jewish context into the wider Hellenistic society, and (b) the fact that that society in turn was characterized by concern for speculative, cosmological questions. Thus for him the philosophical speculation and so the doctrinal-dogmatic form characteristic of traditional Christianity is a "phase" or "stage" of the development of Christianity, and, dependent as it was on a certain cultural setting, this stage has ceased with Christianity's development into the modern world. Adolph von Harnack, *History of Dogma* (New York: Russell & Russell, 1958), Vol. I, Chapter I, paragraph 1; Chapter II, Paragraphs 1,5,6; Vol. II, Chapters IV and VI.

5. This is, of course, the theme of most of Heidegger's thought, but nowhere more clearly than in the book *What Is Called Thinking?* esp. Part II, Lectures III and IV.

6. After Thales' first attempt to comprehend origins in terms of "water," these are the suggestions, respectively, of Empedocles, Heraclitus, Anaximander, Plato, Democritus, and Aristotle. Cf., for fragments representative of these views, Milton C. Nahm, *Selections from Early Greek Philosophy*, 3rd ed. (New York: F. S. Crofts & Co., 1947).

7. "It is clear then that it is the work of one science also to study the things that are, *qua* being. . . . If, then, this is substance, it will be of substances that the philosopher must grasp the principles and the causes" (Aristotle, *Metaphysics*, 1003b, ll. 15–20). "Obviously then it is the work of one science to examine being *qua* being, and the attributes which belong to it *qua* being, and the same science will examine not only substances, but also their attributes . . ." (*Metaphysics*, 1005a, ll. 13–16). "For none of them [qualities, attributes, or actions] is either self-subsistent or capable of being separated from substance, but rather, if anything, it is that which walks or sits or is healthy that is an existing thing. . . . Clearly then it is in virtue of this category that each of the others also *is*. Therefore that which is primarily, i.e. not in a qualified sense but without qualification, must be substance" (*Metaphysics*, 1028a, ll. 28–30). *The Basic Works of Aristotle*, ed. by Richard McKeon (New York: Random House, 1941), pp. 732–83.

Interestingly, Whitehead in our age makes the same correlation between metaphysical philosophy and the principles that characterize existence at its most fundamental level—"what it means for a thing to be"—: "It is the task of philosophy to work at the concordance of ideas conceived as illustrated in the concrete facts of the real world. It seeks those generalities which characterize the complete reality of fact, and apart from which any fact must sink into an abstraction. But science makes the abstraction, and is content to understand the complete fact in respect to only some of its essential aspects. . . . A philosophic system should present an elucidation of concrete fact from which the sciences abstract." A. N. Whitehead, *Adventures of Ideas*, p. 187.

8. For example, cf. the following from Xenophanes (ca. 565–498 B.C.): "But mortals suppose that the gods are born (as they themselves are), and that they wear men's clothing and have human voice and body. But if cattle or lions had hands, so as to paint with their hands and produce works of art as men do, they would paint their gods and give them bodies in form like their own—horses like horses, cattle like cattle. Homer and Hesiod attributed to the gods all things which are disreputable and worthy of blame when done by men; and they told of them many lawless deeds, stealing, adultery, and deception of each other." Fragments 5, 6, and 7, Nahm, *op. cit.*, p. 109. On the contrary, "God is one, supreme among gods and men, and not like mortals in body or in mind. . . . Without effort He sets in motion all things by mind and thought. It [i.e., being] always abides in the same place, not moved at all, nor is it fitting that it should move from one place to another." Fragments 1, 3, and 4, *ibid.* The far greater sense of transcendence, ultimacy, and holiness in the *philosophical* as opposed to the *mythical* conception of God is, it seems to me, unmistakably clear in these earliest "theological" fragments.

For another, later example of this same "prophetic" disdain for the traditional myths as desecrating the goodness and the transcendence of the divine, see Plato's hard-nosed attitude toward poets who delude and misinform people about the gods: *Laws*, Book II, paragraph 659; Book III, paragraph 700; Book VII, paragraphs 801, 817. Over against the desecration of the gods by myth and poetry, Plato places as the spiritual foundation of the community a *valid* "theology" founded on "reasonable evidences," in which the existence and the goodness of the gods is rationally demonstrated and so veridically conceived. Book X, paragraphs 884–906. Cf. also *The Republic*, Book II, 377—Book III, 397. For these citations, see *The Dialogues of Plato*, tr. by B. Jowett (New York: Random House, 1937), Vols. I and II.

9. For a particularly brilliant and informative study of the influence of Greek philosophy on the major theological conceptions of the Christian Fathers, cf. Harry A. Wolfson, *The Philosophy of the Church Fathers* (Cambridge: Harvard University Press, 1956), Vol. I.

10. An extremely helpful discussion of the influence of Greek philosophy on early Christian views of deity—surprisingly sophisticated in its theological insight—is to be found in Robert M. Grant, *The Early Christian Doctrine of God* (Charlottesville: University

Press of Virginia, 1966), esp. Chapter 1 and Appendices I and II. Concrete examples of this influence from the original sources, in Justin Martyr, Irenaeus, Tertullian, Clement, Origen, Athanasius, and Augustine, are too numerous to cite here, and anyway the point since Harnack has hardly been controversial!

11. Although one of the relatively nonphilosophical of the Fathers, Irenaeus nonetheless clearly depends on philosophical concepts of man, of incorruption and of eternity, when he writes about the meaning of even such a unique and miraculous event as the Incarnation; the following reveals the baffling mixture of philosophical and mythical language that is typical of Patristic writers: "Therefore, as I have already said, He [Jesus Christ] caused man (human nature) to cleave to and to become one with God. For unless man had overcome the enemy of man, the enemy would not have been legitimately vanquished. And again: unless it had been God who had freely given salvation, we could never have possessed it securely. And unless man had been joined to God, he could never have become a partaker of incorruptibility." "For it was to this end that the Word of God was made man, and He who was the Son of God, became the Son of Man, that man, having been taken into the Word, and receiving the adoption, might become the son of God. . . . But how could we be joined to incorruptibility and immortality unless, first, incorruptibility and immortality had become that which we also are. . . ?" Irenaeus, *Against Heresies*, Book III, Chapter XVIII and XIX, pp. 448–449, found in *The Anti-Nicene Fathers*, Vol. I.

This passage gives a clue to the later importance, e.g., in Cyril of Alexandria, of the "impersonal humanity" of Jesus Christ, though that doctrine was never implied by Irenaeus: namely, that because Jesus was Man and not merely *a* man, He, in being united to the divine Logos, unites *us* (who as particular men also participate in the universal Man which He embodied) to the divine. Thus it was through an "assist" from Platonism that most of Alexandrian theology understood the efficacy of the Incarnation for the salvation of all men.

12. The paradoxical presence of both a philosophical language that entails the divine universality, self-sufficiency and so holiness, and thus the divine transcendence over time and over all history in time on the one hand, and a mythical language expressive of the divine intentionality and activity in relation to time on the other, is found throughout Augustine whenever he speaks of God's actions in Creation, Providence, Incarnation, or Eschatology. The following *vis-à-vis* Creation is a good example: "Thou, therefore, O Lord, who art not one thing in one place, and otherwise in another, but the Self-same, the Self-same, and the Self-same, Holy, Holy, Holy, Lord God Almighty, didst in the beginning, which is of Thee, in Thy Wisdom, which was born of Thy Substance, create something, and that out of nothing." Augustine, *The Confessions*, Book XII, Chapter VII, in Oates, *op. cit.*, Vol. I, p. 207.

13. The requirement that God, if He is to be a crucial factor in the existence of all things—i.e., of universal and of ultimate signifi-

cance—must be ontologically (metaphysically) conceived as well as postulated as the basis of religious experience, is well put by Whitehead in the following: "It may be doubted whether any properly general metaphysics can ever, without the illicit introduction of other considerations, get much further than Aristotle [i.e., with regard to the nature of God]. But his conclusion does represent a first step without which no evidence on a narrower experiential basis can be of much avail in shaping the conception. For nothing, within any limited type of experience, can give intelligence to shape our ideas of any entity at the base of all actual things, unless the general character of things requires that there be such an entity." A. N. Whitehead, *Science in the Modern World*, pp. 242–43. (The phrase in brackets is added.)

14. The dialectic to which we refer in the relation of philosophy to religion and theology is again well illustrated by Whitehead. In his thought, philosophical explication is essential if the conception of the divine is to be universal and significant enough to be a referent to the *divine*. Nevertheless, he insists that that very metaphysical method is quite unable to rise above the world whose universal structures and factors it is philosophy's task to uncover. Thus—as one "non-Whiteheadian" implication of this argument—*if* the divine is to be in any sense transcendent to the system of the given world, philosophical language must in turn transcend itself into another form of speech. The philosophical alternatives to some such transcendence are apparently to espouse either a monism in which genuine finite contingency and autonomy are lost, as in Spinoza, Hegel, and Bradley, or else to fashion the concept of a finite god, one factor among a series of factors in the total system of things, which was Whitehead's own solution: "Any proof which commences with the consideration of this character of the actual world cannot rise above the actuality of the world. It can only discover all the factors disclosed in the world as experienced. In other words, it may discover an immanent God, but not a God wholly transcendent. The difficulty can be put in this way: by considering the world we can find all the factors required by the total metaphysical situation; but we cannot discover anything not included in this totality of actual fact, and yet explanatory of it." A. N. Whitehead, *Religion in the Making* (New York: The Macmillan Company, 1926), p. 71.

15. Perhaps the best statement in Plotinus of the transcendence of the One to all naming, and so to thought and speech alike, is the following from Ennead V, iii 12–14: "The entire Intellectual Order may be figured as a kind of light with the One in repose at its summit as its King. We may think of the One as a light before the light, an eternal irradiation resting upon the Intellectual; This, not identical with its source, is yet not so remote from It to be less than Real-Being; It is the primal Knower. But the One, as transcending Intellect, transcends knowing. The One is, in truth, beyond all statement; whatever you say would limit It; the All-Transcending, transcending even the most august Mind, which alone of all things has true being, has no name. We can but try to indicate, if possible, something

concerning It. If we do not grasp It by knowledge, that does not mean that we do not seize It at all. We can state what It is not while we are silent as to what It is." *The Essence of Plotinus*, comp. by Grace H. Turnbull, tr. by Stephen Mackenna (New York: Oxford University Press, 1948), p. 162. Cf. also Enneads I, vii, 1; III, viii, 9–10; VI, ix, 3.

16. The principle of "overflow," perhaps the most fundamental ontological principle in Plotinus, is stated in several places in the Enneads: "It is of the essence of things that each gives of its being to another; else the Good would not be Good, nor Divine Mind be Divine Mind, nor Soul be what it is; the law is, some life after the Primal Life, a second where there is a first; all linked in an unbroken chain, all eternal." Ennead, II, ix, 3, *ibid*, p. 64. "The Soul of the All abides in contemplation of the Highest, for ever striving towards the Realm of the Intelligible and towards God; but thus absorbing and filled full, it overflows, so to speak, and the image it gives forth will be the creative puissance. This ultimate phase (of the Soul) then is the Maker. . . ." Ennead II, iii, 18, *ibid.*, p. 62. Cf. also V, i, 6, *ibid.*, p. 158.

The other, closely allied principle explanatory of the relation of the One or the Good to creaturely finite life is even more "mythical," namely, the anxious and fatal "plunge" of the soul into the depths of matter and of relative nonbeing, out of which comes time, life, world, and all suffering and evil: "For the Soul contained an unquiet faculty, always desirous of translating elsewhere what it saw in the Authentic Realm, and it could not bear to retain within itself all the dense fullness of its possession. . . . The nature-principle within, uncoiling outwards, makes its way towards what seems to it a multiple life; it was unity self-gathered, but now, in going forth from itself, it fritters its unity away. . . . To bring this cosmos into being, the Soul first laid aside its eternity and clothed itself with Time. . . ." Ennead III, vii, 11, *ibid.*, p. 106.

"The souls of men . . . have entered into that realm in a leap downward from the Supreme. . . . The ineluctable law is that each soul, according to its rank, is overruled to go towards that to which it characteristically tends, the image of its primal choice . . . to every soul its hour; when that strikes it descends and enters the body suitable to it as at the cry of a herald." Ennead IV, iii, 12–13, *ibid.*, p. 122–23. Cf. also Ennead IV, viii, 4, where such "ontic" or "personal" words as "deserter," "isolated," "wakened," "anxious," "fallen," "burial," "encavernment" are used (*ibid.*, pp. 148–49).

17. Wolfhart Pannenberg has brilliantly argued that the basic principle of divine revelation in Scripture is not the *self*-manifestation of God, so central to neo-orthodoxy, but the *indirect* manifestation of God in and through events in history. Cf. Wolfhart Pannenberg in *Revelation As History* (New York: The Macmillan Company, 1968), the "Introduction" and Chapter IV. "Dogmatic Theses on the Doctrine of Revelation." Whether this thesis (no self-manifestation but only indirect manifestation) can be carried through as totally as Pannenberg wishes, remains doubtful to this writer—but his stress on the important category of indirect manifestation and so on God's acts in

objective or public history is, it seems to me, a real correction to the exclusively subjective or inward-personal locus of revelation in neo-orthodoxy.

18. Cf. this writer's *Maker of Heaven and Earth* for a more detailed discussion of this aspect of the divine "freedom," esp. pp. 96–101.

19. The difficulty a philosophical theology has with special or unique historical events as bearers of ultimately significant redemption and/or truth is, of course, famous, beginning with the deists' rejection of special revelation as "unjust," continuing with Lessing's famous "ditch," and manifesting itself in the present in the difficulties (apparently) process philosophy has with the *Einmaligkeit* of Jesus Christ. For this, cf. Schubert M. Ogden, *Christ Without Myth* (New York: Harper & Row, 1961), esp. pp. 114 ff., 140 ff., 153 ff., where the utter uniqueness and centrality of the event of Christ is qualified as "myth" in favor of its "decisiveness." Cf. the same theme in Van A. Harvey, *The Historian and the Believer* (New York: The Macmillan Company, 1966), Chapters VII and VIII.

Two remarks might be made here on this very complex and important discussion, which, incidentally, Ogden's excellent book has greatly clarified and advanced: (1) The problem is not resolved by pointing out that in *all* his acts God acts "uniquely," i.e., appropriately to each new situation, as Augustine's, Calvin's, Whitehead's, and Hartshorne's God clearly did or does. For if *all* divine acts are unique—as, for example, all men are in this sense unique—this gives to no single one of those acts any overriding authority to be "decisive," i.e., normative, in the interpretation of man's situation in the wider nature of things. Thus the uniqueness of God's act in every historical event by no means establishes or even makes intelligible any decisiveness or authority for the figure of Jesus. If the event of Jesus is to provide or *even be the norm for* (as Ogden wishes to make it, e.g., *ibid.*, p. 138) the fundamental principles by which we interpret ourselves and our relation to God—a relation that is, as Ogden rightly argues, universal—he must *in a different way* be "unique" than are the "ordinary" events to be so interpreted. And this *different* or "unique" sort of uniqueness is (a) difficult for a philosophical theology either to admit or to categorize, and (b) falls precisely into the category of "myth" which is outlawed by Ogden's argument. Cf. *ibid.*, Chapter III and Chapter IV, where myth is defined as a series of assertions about God's acts not translatable exhaustively into assertions about man's self-understanding, e.g., "In Jesus Christ God acted uniquely." Ogden, as well as Bultmann, is here faced with a difficult alternative: (a) if the possibility of authentic existence and with it our understanding of the God whom we universally encounter can be seen, correctly understood, and redemptively appropriated through *all* or even through *many* events, the event of Jesus Christ can by no means be "decisive" for either our self-understanding or for our correlated understanding of God. (b) If, on the other hand, Jesus Christ *is* decisive in any sense—so that there is *"kein andrer Gott,"* as Ogden wishes to maintain (*ibid.*, p. 144)—then inevitably Jesus must have an authority that other events or persons, revealing other things about man and God, do not have; then he is "unique" in a *unique way*, and to make that uniqueness intelligible theologically we must speak of God's unique action in him, i.e., we must speak "mythically." Let us note that this dilemma of a "unique uniqueness" is *not* forced upon us by the issue of salvation in and through the event of Christ, as if by adopting a universalist position (which all of us probably share) we could escape the problem of myth, i.e., of uniqueness and historicity. The same issue is raised by any meaning we might give to the word "decisive," and *a fortiori* when that word is, as in Ogden's thought, given a *normative* meaning. If an event or person is to have normative authority over our interpretation of other events, and if we are to make that status or role *theologically* intelligible, we must recognize in some form its uniqueness in the divine economy of events, i.e., that *God* (as well as we) gives it uniqueness and so normative significance over other events; and expressing in language *that* recognition lands us again in mythical discourse.

(2) If, to escape this use of mythical language, we affirm that the principles by which we interpret our existence and God are *not* either to be provided or to be normatively judged by this event, then they must be provided or assessed—not only in possibility but in actuality—in terms of some *other* event, or, at best, in terms of the universal character of *all* events, and so in the latter case by a natural theology. In such a case, Jesus, having no unique authority, embodies only what can in fact be known elsewhere (not what *could* be known elsewhere), and thus *what* he manifests is determined by the criteria and the content drawn from the known character of all events. General experience is here the norm, and so it is that general experience, and not he that is "decisive"—there is here *"kein andrer Gott"* than some assessment of *general experience* will sanction and allow. At most Jesus is here one of many examples of these general principles evident in all of experience. But then it is difficult to see what the word "decisive" means theologically in relation to Jesus, and why there is *"kein andrer Gott"* than *he* manifests.

In sum, whatever difficulties with mythical language the "right wing" of Bultmann interpreters may have had, there is, we maintain, no possibility of the Left wing alternative that Ogden proposes (*ibid.*, pp. 96–98, 146–64), that is, an intelligible theology based on a "decisive" event and yet quite free of mythological language. If the event is decisive, i.e., normative, for the self-understanding of man and the correlated understanding of God, then mythical discourse (to be sure, pruned, as Bultmann also insisted, of matters-of-fact statements and correlated with existential relation to the symbols) is essential to its intelligible theological explication.

20. The mixture of philosophical and mythical forms of language in Christian theology has traditionally been more pervasive than in Judaism, although Philo and Maimonides surely illustrate it as well. The reason, possibly, is that while Judaism is surely as "particular-

istic" and as "historical" as Christianity, finding its unique sources in the events and life of a particular history, it has generally not wished to assert in the same way the claim to universality, that is, to represent the way in which all men should believe, worship, and so be saved. Hence it has not been driven so inexorably to express that universality in the universalizing categories of philosophical explication.

21. The intractable difficulties in the Whiteheadian understanding of God—is He *an* entity or a route of entities, and how are we categorially to understand the *everlastingness* of His being as well as the *relatedness* of His being to the world—not only represent the reverse difficulties of the traditional theistic understanding of God in terms of Greek philosophy, but even more indicate that a *unique* being or factor in the universe, explanatory of its harmony as a *whole*, cannot be understood in precisely the univocal terms with which we understand "ordinary" beings, but must be understood analogically and mythically.

22. The phenomenal concreteness of the divine activity in history was surely characteristic of Hebrew faith, where actual political events in the nation's history were regarded as the work of God—often, when they were particularly bloody conquests, to the discomfort of later commentators! In Christian tradition the same phenomenal concreteness was established in the Docetic controversy in which the Incarnate Word or Logos of God was, paradoxically, described also as being a particular man of actual flesh and bone, with real needs and a painful death.

23. The best, and most important, example of the combination of mythical and philosophical language in theological statement is the Chalcedonian Creed, in which the theme of the "story" of the descent of a divine being is united with the conception of a union of two "natures." In this creedal statement, phrases the meanings of which are derived from the philosophical categories used, e.g., "consubstantial with," "in two natures," and so on, are combined with phrases indicating that a divine being (the Son of God or the Logos), who had been "begotten by the Father before all ages," had now "in the last days" descended and been born of the Virgin for our salvation, which phrases are clearly "mythic" in form and meaning, portraying as they do the activity of a transcendent being in entering the space-time world for our salvation.

24. The most persuasive form of these arguments is, we feel, found in the writings of A. N. Whitehead, and our remarks are largely patterned after his elaboration of them. Cf. *The Function of Reason* (Princeton: Princeton University Press, 1929), pp. 29 f. and 51 f.; *Adventures of Ideas*, pp. 182–85, 255–56, 280; *Process and Reality*, pp. 150 f., 500–502; *Modes of Thought*, pp. 145–46.

25. Auguste Comte, *The Positive Philosophy*, tr. by Harriet Martineau, 3rd ed. (London: Kegan Paul, Trench, Trübner & Company, 1893), Vol. I, Chapter I; Vol. II, Chapters VII, IX, X, XIII–XV.

26. The relation of philosophical to other forms of inquiry as their

foundation and so their "critic," is well spelled out in the following famous quotation from Whitehead: "I hold that philosophy is the critic of abstractions. Its function is the double one, first of harmonising them by assigning to them their right relative status as abstractions, and secondly, of completing them by direct comparison with more concrete intuitions of the universe, and thereby promoting the formation of more complete schemes of thought. . . . Philosophy is not one among the sciences with its own little scheme of abstractions which it works away at perfecting and improving. It is the survey of the sciences, with the special objects of their harmony, and of their completion. It brings to this task, not only the evidence of the separate sciences, but also its own appeal to concrete experience. It confronts the sciences with concrete fact." *Science and the Modern World*, p. 122. The same assertion that philosophy is the surveyor and the judge of other, more special modes of language is, interestingly enough, made by linguistic philosophy, only now not on the basis that philosophy provides a means of knowing "concreteness" (i.e., what is really actual) more directly than do the sciences, but rather that it represents a mode of analysis of the grammar, usages, and so the interrelations of the language games of the various sciences. No better expression in academia of the "secularity" of our culture can be found than in the fact that few if any persons involved in the "special" sciences recognize the need of their science for any such philosophical foundations, whether of a metaphysical or a linguistic sort.

27. As our first and second chapters argued, the important interrelationships of science and theology are both undeniable and unavoidable. If this be so, then they cannot, as neo-orthodoxy hoped, each proceed on its own separate path as if the other were not there at all, for alone and in isolation neither one can fully understand its own development. Thus some form of mediation through ontology is unavoidable. For the important modes of reverse influence that *theology* has had on the development of modern science, cf. this writer's *Maker of Heaven and Earth*, Chapter 5.

28. A more thorough analysis of these other, noncognitive experiences of ultimacy in ordinary life is to be found in *Naming the Whirlwind*, Part II, Chapters 2, 3, and 4.

29. Perhaps the major doctrinal criticism this writer would make of the new eschatological theology of Jürgen Moltmann (though not of Pannenberg) is (1) that he seems to juxtapose as opposites Providence and Eschatology, the work of God in the past and present, and the coming work of God in the future, and (2) consequently he seeks to speak *only* of the future activity of God. This, it seems to me, is to isolate the "new" in the future, and the God who is to bring it in, so radically from the present that it makes unintelligible not only (a) how we can now know anything of God and His promises, but even more (b) how that future new can have any intelligible and so redemptive relation to the *current* social structures of economic and political injustice which our own and God's actions are supposed in the coming time to redeem. For a more detailed form of this

critique, cf. my essay, "The Contribution of Culture to the Reign of God," in Maryellen Muckenhirn, ed., *The Future As the Presence of Shared Hope* (New York: Sheed and Ward, 1968), pp. 34–58.

30. In the issue of *Daedalus* already referred to (Summer, 1967, Vol. 96, No. 3), a group of very distinguished students of technology and of human society (sociologists, anthropologists, psychologists, etc.) sought to "predict" the character of our society in the year 2000. This awestruck reader noted several characteristics of these predictions: (1) Most were based on the presupposition that present dominant or "long-term" (!) trends would continue (e.g., Herman Kahn and A. Wiener, p. 706). Clearly this presupposition (or tautology) in turn assumed without even any discussion an answer to one *very* significant question about the character of that future, namely, whether or not it will be characterized by fundamental changes from our present situation. For presumably the meaning of *radical* change is precisely that such changes dissolve even our most cherished "long-term trends." Without such an assumption of the basic continuity of current trends and so, on the basis of that continuity, of the continuing meaning and relevance of figures currently available to us, no "scientific" prediction apparently would be possible, and presumably someone like Ezekiel would have to be called in. Whether this assumption about continuities in the future is itself "scientific" or not—and what on earth it might *mean* to call it "scientific"—or whether (which is surely more relevant) such an assumption is even historically probable, are interesting questions to which no answers, nor even any attention, were here given.

(2) Almost all the political and sociological writers presupposed as the other major invariable around which to build their pictures of the future the continuing existence of a "free society." That is to say, what they seem to have been doing was (a) to assume, as noted above, the continuity of certain basic current trends, and (b) then to imagine what in those circumstances a free society like ours would be like. I noted with some relief that this second presupposition, alike adopted without discussion or debate, assumed a comforting answer to perhaps the *other* pressing question anxious mortals raise about our future, namely, whether or not a free society of some sort will continue as the murky future unfolds.

(3) The predictions were made, apparently, without any general, preliminary discussion about the character of historical process as such. Thus no preliminary clarification, much less agreement, was achieved on the crucial question of the relative influence on historical change of the various relevant factors (technological, political, economic, moral, ideological, etc.). *A fortiori* no mention was made of the further question of the relative influence of determination and of freedom in history, or, to make this point more concrete, of the relative significance of impersonal social and historical forces as opposed to intentional or rational "choices." Needless to say, both of these are matters extremely relevant to the questions of the methodology and even the viability of prediction. In other words, the nature

of historical process, which process represented the *very field* within which the predictions were being made, was never even broached as a serious problem for reflection. Thus, even granting the viability or rationality of assuming the two very question-begging presuppositions mentioned above, no *theoria* or rational (read "scientific") understanding was offered concerning the relative status or effectiveness of the various forms of continuity that were in fact assumed. The added fact that historians and philosophers (not to mention theologians!) were noticeably absent—although presumably they were men who have thought somewhat about continuities and discontinuities, variables and invariables in history, and what the influential factors in historical change might in fact be—adds to this impression of the fundamental *irrationality* of the effort of "scientific futurology" as now assayed. Like so much else in our culture, in its effort to be "objective" and so "scientific," current futurology remains shut within the limited abstractions of each specialized field, and thus does not even uncover, much less demonstrate, its own basic assumptions. In the sense that these assumptions (as noted above) were by no means obvious, often apparently and probably sanguine, and certainly unclarified, the whole effort seemed less rationally grounded than the earlier types of prophecy based as they were on the rationale of the divine faithfulness to the divine promises!

In any case, Donald A. Schon is thus probably right when he says that "We see forecasts as tools or aids for decision rather than assertions about the future" (*ibid.*, p. 769); and so is Andrew Shonfield when he calls such predictions a modern form of the literary art of "utopia-building" in which more is revealed about what the author thinks our present social priorities should be than about the shape of the actual future. (Andrew Shonfield, "Thinking About the Future," in *Encounter*, Vol. XXXII, No. 2, February, 1969, pp. 15–26.) Apparently, for the twentieth century its future destiny remains as mysterious as that destiny did in older times, since even our most quantitative, and so scientific predictions, can address themselves to the question of how much discontinuity will appear in that future only by begging that very question. Further, it is apparent that the effort to *understand* the problem of destiny cannot even be rationally and so "scientifically" assayed unless we move beyond the level of mere fact, statistics, and current "dominant trends" to a consideration of the nature of historical process itself, that is, to the level of philosophical and theological symbolization.

31. The main difficulty with a purely Biblical eschatological discussion of destiny, as carried on for example by Moltmann, *op. cit.*, and by Carl Braaten in *The Future of God* (New York: Harper & Row, 1969), is the reverse of the one mentioned in the preceding footnote, namely, that they omit entirely from their discussion of destiny questions of the concrete processes of present social history, questions to be answered by empirical studies of technology and its possibilities, current social changes and trends, probable developments in political life and their potential direction, and so on. Such theologies

unfold, therefore, a philosophy of history—for that is what it is—solely out of the Biblical symbols themselves, and thus they lack all concrete historical content whatsoever. This is, of course, to presuppose that what now is—in technology, social and political structures, intellectual and moral ideas and values, and so on—will have *no* influence at all on what will be. But if *that* is the case, then one wonders what these authors mean by their call to us now to "obedience" and so to "revolution" in order to humanize and so to redeem the oppressive and unjust social structures that now surround us. Surely *both* the present shape of those social structures, *and* the present character of our decisions and acts, are relevant to the shape of any new world that we or the Lord are to bring in—in which case the character of that new, and so the contents of our hopes, and thus *a fortiori* the way we talk about destiny, are *in part* to be determined by these concrete historical movements in which we and God are to be at work, but which are to be known and talked about in terms of the "secular" disciplines of technological studies, social sciences, and history.

Index